Us&Them

MUSLIM–CHRISTIAN RELATIONS AND CULTURAL HARMONY IN AUSTRALIA

Abe W. Ata

First published in 2009 from a completed manuscript presented to
Australian Academic Press
32 Jeays Street
Bowen Hills Qld 4006
Australia
www.australianacademicpress.com.au

Copyright © 2009 Abe Ata and the listed co-authors.

All responsibility for editorial matter rests with the authors. Any views or opinions expressed are therefore not necessarily those of Australian Academic Press.

Reproduction and communication for educational purposes:
The Australian Copyright Act 1968 (the Act) allows a maximum of one chapter or 10% of the pages of this work, whichever is the greater, to be reproduced and/or communicated by any educational institution for its educational purposes provided that the educational institution (or the body that administers it) has given a remuneration notice to Copyright Agency Limited (CAL) under the Act.

For details of the CAL licence for educational institutions contact:
Copyright Agency Limited
Level 19, 157 Liverpool Street
Sydney NSW 2000
Australia
Telephone: (02) 9394 7600
Facsimile: (02) 9394 7601
E-mail: info@copyright.com.au

Reproduction and communication for other purposes:
Except as permitted under the Act (for example, a fair dealing for the purposes of study, research, criticism or review) no part of this book may be reproduced, stored in a retrieval system, communicated or transmitted in any form or by any means without prior written permission. All inquiries should be made to the publisher at the address above.

National Library of Australia cataloguing-in-publication entry:

Author:	Ata, Abe W.
Title:	Us & them : Muslim-Christian relations and cultural harmony in Australia / Abe Ata.
Edition:	1st ed.
ISBN:	9781921513190 (pbk.)
Subjects:	Religion and sociology--Australia. Islam--Relations--Christianity--Australia. Christianity and other religions--Islam--Australia. Australia--Emigration and immigration.
Dewey Number:	261.270994

This work is dedicated to my friend Steven Klimidis who passed away on August 26, 2008. Dr Klimidis was a pioneer in transcultural psychiatry in Australia and an Associate Professor at the Victorian Transcultural Psychiatry Unit — a truly generous, humble and passionate person.

Contents

Acknowledgments	vii
About the Author	viii
Introduction	1

Section One: Cross-Religious and Cultural Attitudes

Chapter 1
Cross-Religious Misunderstanding
or a Clash Between Civilisations in Australia — 7

Chapter 2
Christian–Muslim Households Identity
and Attitudes to Their 'Australian' Children — 19

Chapter 3
Attitudes of School-Age Non-Muslim Australians
Towards Muslims and Islam: A National Survey — 33

Chapter 4
The Lebanese in Melbourne Ethnicity, Interethnic Activities
and Attitudes to Australia — 45

Section Two: Education

Chapter 5
The Role of Gender, Religion and Friendship in the Perception
of the 'Other' — An Investigation of Secondary Students
in Australia: A National Survey — 65

Chapter 6
The Role of Australian Schools in Educating Students
About Islam and Muslims: A National Survey
(co-authored with Joel Windle) — 81

Chapter 7
Social Distance From Muslims: A National Survey — 99

Chapter 8
Attitudes of School-Age Muslim Australians Towards
Australia — Gender and Religious Differences
A National Survey — 111

Section Three: Muslim–Christian Intermarriage

Chapter 9
Adjustment and Complications of Christian–Muslim
Intermarriages in Australia — 127

Chapter 10
Bereavement Anxieties and Health
Among the Arab Muslim Community — 145

Chapter 11
Observing Different Faiths, Learning About Ourselves
Practice With Intermarried Muslims and Christians
(co-authored with Mark Furlong) — 157

Chapter 12
Opting for an Eschatological Interpretation
of Interfaith Marriages
(co-authored with Glenn Morrison) — 173

Acknowledgments

I wish to thank several people for their support of this publication, particularly Professor Robert Gascoigne. Others include Professor Abdullah Saeed, Dr Hass Dellal AOM, Ramzi Elsayed, Roberta Blake and Maureen Postma. Support from the Department of Immigration and Citizenship (DIAC) is proudly acknowledged. DIAC's support enabled me to produce two national surveys on attitudes of school-age Muslim–Australians to Australia; and, attitudes of non-Muslim school-age Australians to Muslims and Islam. Reference to these surveys is found in several chapters of this publication.

About the Author

Abe W. Ata graduated at the American University of Beirut in 1972 and in 1980 completed his PhD at the University of Melbourne. In 1970 he was nominated as a delegate to the United Nations in New York.

Dr Ata has taught in Australian, American, Jordanian, West Bank and Danish universities. As well, he convened and directed the Victorians For Racial Equality in 1985; and Al-Quds University Centre of Traumatic Studies in 1997.

There are 94 articles and 15 books to his credit including *Religion and Ethnic Identity: An Australian Study, Vols. 1–3* (1989–1990), *The West Bank Family* (London, Routledge, 1986), *The Ethnic Press in Australia* (Academia Press, 1990), *Bereavement and Health in Australia* (1996), *Christian and Muslim Intermarriage* (London, Routledge, 2001), *Australia's Christian–Muslim Intermarriage* (Melbourne, 2003), *Australia's Catholic and Other Faith Intermarriages* (Melbourne, 2005).

The Encyclopaedia of Melbourne (2005), the *Encyclopaedia Australian People* (2000) and the *Encyclopaedia of Australian Religions* (2009) include several of his contributions.

Dr Ata is a Senior Associate Fellow at the Australian Catholic University.

Introduction

It is not a recent phenomenen that mistrust of Muslims by Western countries is rooted in a perception that the modern scourge of terrorism stems from a religious basis. As far back as 1995, the Oklahoma City bombing on April 19 that killed 168 people immediately sparked a search for Islamic terrorists. Although the culprits were extremists bent on creating terror, they were not Muslims but rather US-born anti-government 'survivalists' who were angry with the US government. The initial belief that the attack was organised by a group of Muslim terrorists was repeated on several national television networks.

Research indicates that Australian–Muslims have surpassed Asians as one of Australia's most marginalised religious and ethnic groups. ABC Radio National's *The World Today* program (February 19, 2003) revealed that more than any other cultural or ethnic group, Muslims and people from the Middle East are thought to be unable to fit into Australia, with more than 50% of Australians preferring their relatives did not to marry into a Muslim family; and that Australia was weakened because they were 'sticking to their old ways'.

Without doubt this is an oversimplification of diverse interpretations of interfaith relations and cultural harmony — one that makes it difficult for an outsider to come up with a legitimate single truth.

It is important to consider the patterns of cross-cultural differences, as one becomes confused and reactive when communicating with participants in the field. This is a challenge in a society like Australia that contains a multitude of cultures with diverse points of view.

In communicating with participants from several cultures, the responses may reflect different world views in the way they are affected by outside events. One participant rescheduled an interview several times, each time insisting that I meet at another convenient time. When I insisted that he commit himself in earnest, he grumbled, 'Inshallah' — God willing. Finally, he apologised that he had no time. Some who agreed to the interview often increased the volume of their conversation as a sign that a loud voice makes a sound argument.

in their classrooms. They highlight key issues, generate new questions and critiques, make observations, and provide extensive annotated bibliographies for multicultural literature.

A number of these essays explore the need for new content and procedures in creating an 'anti-bias' curriculum and discusses ways to create an anti-bias environment, learn about differences, teach about differences, and resist stereotyping students.

Having stated the above, the reader is reminded that the phrase 'non-Muslim Australians' is not restricted to Christians, even though the book deals overwhelmingly with Australian Christian and Muslim communities.

The first chapter, 'Cross-Religious Misunderstanding, or a Clash Between Civilisations in Australia', is about racial tensions between immigrant Muslims and white Australia. It presents the grievances and general perspectives of the Muslim community and the Australian Christian community towards each other. It recognises that the wide cultural and historical differences between the two communities are too wide to reconcile, but given the alternatives, a creative dialogue must continue. Ultimately, each community must ask: How are we going to portray a better image of the other community?

Chapter 2 presents the common expectations, disagreements and the sense of destiny that parents in mixed Muslim–Christian marriages hold towards their children. The findings can be viewed as the seeds of change from the way previous generations from particular religious-ethnic backgrounds identify themselves.

Chapter 3 reports some results from a large-scale study of attitudes towards Muslims among Australian secondary students. The findings show Australian students are generally ignorant about Muslims and Islam. The chapter poses many challenging questions. If the degree to which students feel that their school is educative about Muslims is an important predictor of certain levels of tolerance, it is the supportive atmosphere created by a school that is educative of Muslims, rather than the level of knowledge about prejudice. Chapter 4 argues that the enormous differences between aspects of the Australian and Lebanese cultures are important factors in creating negative attitudes towards Australia.

Chapter 5 reveals that widespread negative stereotypes among female students tend to suggest that they may not be well informed, while the long-standing multicultural posture of educational policy suggests otherwise. While students agree that the acceptance of Muslims does not come easily in Australia, school does not emerge as a site for change. The findings show that a sizeable proportion of non-Muslim Australian students are ignorant about Muslims and Islam, and few believe that schools are filling the gaps in their knowledge.

Chapter 6 combines findings from boys and girls and reaches several conclusions, including that school is not seen by many as promoting cultural harmony.

Researchers interested in cross-cultural research have come up with exceptional insights into the hopes and fears of dealing with people different to ourselves. As with these researchers, I have realised that my biases and prejudices towards other ethnic and religious minorities are not greatly different to theirs. The list is amazingly similar, and includes fears of being misunderstood, being monitored and judged by government agencies, hurting others unintentionally, miscommunication, and exposing awkward hang-ups and dislikes.

The essays in this book offer some truths as they are believed and expressed by Muslim and non-Muslim Australians. They are interdisciplinary and varied in topic, but generally seek to challenge the images of Islam held by both xenophobic Westerners and extremist Muslims. Several of these essays rehash old territory, but make useful summaries for non-experts. The introductory essay, for example, offers the challenging viewpoint that both Islam and democracy are compatible, irreconcilable and are based on human equality. They also raise thematic questions, such as: What implications do the findings have on us and our community? Will any dialogue lead to a rapprochement between the Muslim and mainstream communities? What is Christian–Muslim diversity? Why does it matter? Can we really learn how to manage diversity in the workplace? Can the Shari'a law coexist with the Australian legal system on issues that include polygamy, marital status and dress?

In the melting pot we call Australia, given that most migrants bring their cultures and the traditions that help to shape their identity, should these people be expected to conform and assimilate, or can we continue to live in a multicultural society? Should they have to leave their culture behind, or preserve it so it can be passed down to their children and grandchildren?

Must Islam first undergo important political and economic developments before it can have a democratic future? Should Islam progress into a separation between clerical and political powers (an essential component of growth in western societies) to be able to compete on the same social, political and economic playing fields?

Intercultural and interfaith education in Australia has been transformed, refocused, and is in a constant state of evolution both in theory and in practice. Clearly, separation between cultural and religious dictates is a key to understanding the Muslim communities at large. For example, the hijab, a cloth that is worn around the head of a Muslim woman, is often misunderstood as a way to keep women hidden and inferior to men. However, wearing the hijab is a voluntary decision. Not all Muslim women decide to wear it.

This volume comprises 12 essays connecting literacy scholarship and theory, reflection, popular culture, politics, history, psychology, contemporary youth issues, canonical, and multicultural works to provide ideas for teachers to use

Students do not seem to perceive their own ignorance as the main difficulty facing Muslims in society. Chapter 7 explores the notion of social distance and how individuals are able to recognise how others are both similar and different from them in forming social attitudes.

Chapter 8 examines the social distance of non-Muslim–Australian students. Having a friend who is Muslim is significantly associated with reduced prejudice towards Muslims. It is suggested that future research examines the sorts of attitudes and beliefs that students hold, and in this way try to understand the psychology behind prejudicial beliefs towards Muslims and Islam.

Chapter 9 forms part of an investigation of Christian–Muslim relationships in Australia. It studies over 100 couples who have married across this religious divide, using religious affiliation as the principal characteristic that defines intermarriage. The problems, pitfalls, joys and pleasures associated with religious intermixing set against a spectrum of parental, communal and affiliates of larger ethnoreligious organisations are portrayed in detail. Chapter 10 falls outside of the main thrust of this section but is nevertheless unique in its diagnosis of the traumas and healing processes interconnected with religious and cultural undercurrents. The study specifically examines the health, ethnic, gender, age and psychological dimensions of bereaved Muslims in Victoria, and makes comparative findings with other cultural and religious communities.

Chapter 11 offers practitioners ideas for working with clients from mixed faith relationships. Several patterns of adaptation of a mixed faith marriage are identified with key questions framed for further analysis. A key question is: How might practitioners position themselves with respect to asymmetries related to gender? Rather than the practitioners seeking to be experts on 'the other', the belief animating the current contribution is the idea that working with diverse clients offers workers a mirror on which we can better observe our own outlines.

Chapter 12 looks at the dynamics of mixed marriage from a fresh unique eschatological perspective. Intermarriage implies the crossing of ethnic, linguistic, religious, racial or national boundaries by a woman and a man in life's most intimate union. The crossing may well be filled with trauma, overwhelming surprises and persecution. Only dialogue — words and meetings — will achieve what is indeed possible. But human life is paradoxical and mysterious. We are not just content with what is possible. We want to be great and achieve the impossible. To go beyond dialogue in the context of an interfaith marriage ruptures the idea of 'the self' and its tendency to be 'for itself'.

Section One

Cross-Religious and Cultural Attitudes

Chapter 1

Cross-Religious Misunderstanding
or a Clash Between Civilisations in Australia

Australia displays an outstanding record, perhaps beyond any other multicultural society, in displaying tolerance and accommodating an incredibly diverse population.

As the Australian community continues to look for ways to mount an inclusive action on behalf of the common good, it takes time to appreciate all the diversities and discover common values between Christians and Muslims. Clearly, the cultural and historical differences between Christian and Muslim communities in our society are too wide to effect a complete reconciliation but, given the alternatives, a creative dialogue must continue. Just like mixed marriages, certain differences between the two faiths may be identified without being fully reconciled. A starting point towards this end is identifying misconceptions, misgivings and the roots of grievances.

Grievances of the Australian Muslim Community

A number of groups — church social justice committees, the Victorian Equal Opportunity Board, the Australian Arabic Council of Victoria, the Islamic Council, the Executive Council of Australian Jewry in Sydney, and some journalists — have observed that the patterns of harassment against the Muslim community have not emerged suddenly. These organisations, and others, have repeatedly voiced their concerns about instances of racial prejudice, long before the events in the Gulf in the early 1990s.

At a local level, examples of reported personal harassment and media bias have been common. The newsletter *Migration Action* of the Ecumenical Migration Centre (April, 1991) reported vandalisation of several Muslim schools and places of worship. Police were also notified of stolen reference books and computer software. Associated damage in some instances involved burnt carpets and broken glass.

Harassment in the street and schoolyard have involved name calling and slurs, abuse, pulling headscarves from women's heads, spitting, refusal of housing and accommodation, telephone or mail threats, graffiti on houses, and throwing of dirty water on women wearing traditional dress in shopping malls.

Many of these kinds of incidents are not officially reported for fear of further harassment, or ignorance of actionable pathways to follow.

Another area of complaint concerns children of Arab-speaking parents. Their grievances relate to a number of issues, one of which occurred during the Gulf War, when many students, including those from a Muslim heritage, were taken to churches to pray for American and Australian troops fighting against Iraq. Muslim parents objected to the fact that such trips were made compulsory and greatly lacking in sensitivity.

In an earlier investigation I found various types of grievances among the local Muslim community, which fall into two main categories.

Split vision: A cultural religious myopia in the media and textbooks

It is generally agreed that reporting on Muslim issues in the local media since the 1970s, and particularly through the recent Palestinian crisis, brought about an atmosphere of religious disharmony. Muslims believe that an in-built bias in Australian reporting makes the context of the events more of a focus than the events themselves. For example, those who fled on epic journeys from extremist regimes are made to carry the stereotype of their leaders. Iraqi refugees and other asylum seekers in detention centres have often been described as 'untrustworthy' or 'genetically terrorists'.

The economic, historical and religious diversity of some 60 Muslim countries are rarely presented. Usually, images portray Muslims as bland, simple, manageable, and an inferior entity. One example is the portrayal of Muslim countries as 'oil-rich', while many, such as the Sudan, Yemen and Gaza are extremely impoverished.

A major study of Victorian schools (Ata & Batrouney, 1989) showed that the type of school attended correlated with the degree of stereotyping. Private school students were more likely to accept negative stereotypes of Muslims and Arabs. The study involved the application of words such as 'rude', 'rich', 'intelligent', 'aggressive', 'lecherous' and 'primitive'. The study found that the absence of both comprehensive relevant curriculum material, and teachers with complete insight into both cultures, were primary factors in the degree of stereotyping that occurred.

Almost 23 years later, tension was fuelled by an incident of gang rape in Sydney involving Australian–Lebanese Muslim youths. The media and leaders of the Muslim community were quick to provide their own version of analysis. *The Age* (Bone, 2002) published two main feature articles carrying opposing views. The first, titled, 'Some Muslim leaders need to realise multiculturalism is a two-way street', argued that 'racially motivated rape, the intention of which is to defile the women of the enemy, is as old as warfare, but it is devastating to think that this could be happening in Australia today' (p. 15). The writer, a female journalist, is stunned that the divide between some Muslim beliefs and the secular Australian culture is so deep. The article points out that the media have been accused of 'breeding hatred by identifying the ethnicity and religion of the rapists. But the rapists themselves identified these as the motivating factor. [Subsequently] the media would not be fulfilling their purpose if they covered up this fact for fear of offending some communities' (p. 15).

The second article by Bloug (2002), 'The media's obsession with race sheds no light on crime', presented an opposing view that the 'stone-throwers' present 'the culture' of the rapists as being a relevant cause of the criminal behaviour. The writer poses the following: 'Now which culture is that? The Muslims? But most Muslims are not Arabs such as in our nearest neighbour Indonesia. The Lebanese? But about half of the Lebanese are Christians. The Arabs? But the offenders are home-grown Australians' (p. 1).

Ironically, proportionally few of the educated community take any steps to remedy the situation. Efforts to promote harmony on talk-back radio, in letters to the editor, book reviews, films, comedy festivals, public debates, or photographic displays are almost non-existent. The question of why there are no people within the Muslim and Arab communities who are able to project a human face in Australia remains a moot point.

Middle-Eastern Christians

What Australians see as a monolithic community is in fact a disparate assemblage of religions and traditions, including Copts, Maronites, Assyrians, Druze, Chaldeans, Melkites, Jews and sundry Christians: 20 million souls in all. They have lived in the Middle East since the Flood. They speak Arabic but are not Muslims. At least in Australia, most of these minorities rarely identify themselves as Arabs. Most of them believe — as do other Australians — that identity is self-defined. Why then would they speak up about the behaviour of one errant cleric who is from another country, another religion, another culture, another world? Some Arab Muslim academics have offered a simplistic politics of identity. They maintain that the Arabic language is an identity marker and that being born in the Middle East results in a new form of Arab creation. They would be puzzled by the reply that just as the German language is not the province of Germans alone, neither is Arabic restricted to Arabs. Like

English, the Arabic language spread through conquests; minorities had to adopt it to survive.

There is a misleading consensus among Arabists that Arab identity rests on religion: that is, that of Islam.

Like Eastern European Christians, the Christian Arab community is subsumed under the flag of Western Christianity. For instance, in any religious dialogues between Judaism, Islam and Christianity, their distinct identity, experiences and character is immediately subsumed under the one Western-coined label of 'Christianity'.

An expert on minorities, Bloul (2002) makes a similar point when she refers to academics who 'seem to think that some of the major obstacles (to integration) come from the various Muslim communities themselves, or more properly from the particularistic (ethnic, national, sectarian) ties within' (p. 1) these communities. She is right to be sceptical about this argument.

Other reports tend to ignore the existence of 15 million Christian Arabs who have lived in Muslim-controlled regimes since the birth of Christ. The existence of such people in Egypt, Palestine, Lebanon, Iraq and other Muslim countries has been ignored in many of the textbooks used in secondary and primary schools.

People promoting sentiments of a monoreligious and monocultural Australia may be motivated by a kind of loyalty, but they are hindering the development of a newly emerging Australian identity. This new identity will come to see Muslim–Australians to be like Catholic–Australians, Italian–Australians, Irish–Australians; that is, both Muslim and Australian.

Examples from the media show a Muslim community that is viewed as one whose culture is diametrically opposite to the mainstream society. The differences are marked by the refusal of the community to come to terms with the Anglo-Saxon mores — mores of a Western culture that defines it as 'rational, developed, humane and superior'. The former, by contrast, is 'psychotic, unbalanced, skilled only at self-defeating rhetoric. It is something to be feared and controlled'.

Grievances of the Australian Christian Community

Clear-thinking Australians point out that whatever wall exists between the Muslim and Christian worlds, it has been built by both sides. It is a wall that is founded on values and ideals that two groups of people hold in their heads. This cultural wall has existed for a long time. With an increase in migration from Muslim countries, whereby the Muslim religion has become the third-largest in the country, the wall has increased in height and influence.

As the two communities have become wary of each other, the government's multicultural initiatives are seeds waiting to take root. Despite initiatives to integrate all of the migrant communities and their overall views and decisions into the mainstream society, a few individuals are unable or unwilling to draw the fine line between Muslim Australians and Muslims living overseas. In a letter to the editor of *The Age* (2002) a reader asks,

> Re 'Palestinian killed on the way to prayers' (*World*, 3/6/2002), is it normal for a Muslim to carry a gun to the mosque to pray? Last month a church in Pakistan was the scene of a bloody attack where an American diplomat and her daughter were killed. Churches in the Philippines are also targets for terror. Clearly to Islamic 'terrorists', a synagogue or church is not a holy ground. (p. 14)

There was no reference in the letter to an Australian 'self-identified' Christian who set fire to the Muslims' second holiest shrine in east Jerusalem two decades earlier.

Others note that Australia, like other English-speaking countries, presses its 'Christian' values for individual and women's rights, and religious freedom of worship, but continues to support authoritarian regimes in supplying weapons and technology. The leaders in Canberra talk to Muslim rulers — not to the people — about where they are heading in the future and how they can work and live together.

In Australia, the separation between the religious and secular identities is a cultural and political given. The community may have been influenced by Christian values but, unlike citizens of Muslim countries, their identity is not exchangeable with a religious affiliation. Muslim participants in this study identified with their particular religious group, but few Christian partners did.

Social commentators have expressed serious reservations about ethnic diversity. One such radio talkback program asked a prominent academic,

> We have secularised Australia and made our religions a private matter ... Why is it when we deal with certain incoming communities we are required to deal with their religious beliefs or religious leaders? ... They may have a larger influence on members of their community than their secular leaders. But we are not dealing with foreign countries here.

Another asked, 'If Laden, a spiritual leader, does not represent true Islam, who does represent true Islam? Will the real Islam stand up?' This is the kind of question that our military and diplomatic institutions are designed never to ask and never to notice they are not asking (Miles, 2002).

The polarised sexual attitudes between the sexually restrictive Muslim communities and a permissive Australian society is a major factor that perpetuates a volatile cultural divide.

A rigid code of honour of males (*ird*) for first-generation Muslims continues to affect what women wear, what they see, places they are not to go, who they mix with, how early they are to return home, what permissive issues they are not to engage in within or outside their own community, which places of entertainment involving drinking and dancing they are to avoid, and why they should not take part in mixed gym or aquatic activities.

For parents it is inconceivable that their daughter would want to dress like other 'parent-absent' Australian girls and make herself sexually attractive. 'Why should she exhibit her charms if she does not mean to sell or give them away?' is a popular question that illustrates the conservative mindset of many parents within an ethnic community (Ata, 1980).

Like other migrant communities, Muslim families increasingly believe they should not feel under pressure to give up their identity, and that their traditional family structure should not be eroded.

To Australian society, composed of both Anglo and non-Anglo Australian-born, expressions of opinion and criticism of their lifestyle is synonymous with separation and antagonism — definitely not to be tolerated. Studies describing the attitudes of first-generation migrants towards Australia are sporadic and few.

In one study, the differences between the predominantly Australian 'Christian' culture and Arab 'Muslim' culture were cited as a major factor in creating negative reactions towards Australia by the latter community (Ata, 1980). Responses relating to sexual permissiveness (19%), unfriendliness (29%) and lack of spiritual values (27%) constituted the bulk of replies. As one participant remarked,

> We give them [the Australians] our hand to shake, and to become friends. Their eyes open instead, thinking we don't want to touch them ... You know what I mean, don't you? Friendship with Australians is easy to make, easy to lose. We have tried the lot ... We invite them to our house, they never show up ... and if we talk to them they open the door a little but they never let you in ... still it is their country. (p. 274)

It is true the above comments are manifestations of a culture shock that most migrants experience when values of the host culture are perceived to contradict those of a traditional social upbringing. In such societies, where informal modes of communication current across civil, official, legal, departmental and institutional spheres of the culture, one's private affairs are considered to be of public interest.

The clear-cut separation between business and pleasure in societies like Australia leaves traditional migrant families baffled. Some criticised a lack of family ties and the upbringing of Australian children. One parent in the same study said,

When their [Australian] children begin to earn money they don't know their parents any more. So they take drugs, drink and bludge around ... or they form gangs and tease everyone in the street ... Don't worry, my girl is doing the same now. She always wants to do things privately and be by herself ... (p. 274)

In highlighting the double standards that some migrant males exhibit within their community, an Australian doctor of Lebanese background observed,

Our men convey an impression of decency and religiosity by sheltering their wives at home ... In the most secret circumstances, they continue to seek treatment for venereal diseases that they have obtained from 'places of entertainment' ... Their wives become infected as a result, and the repercussions are obvious — severe infection or divorce. (p. 34)

Of the 60 ethnic newspapers surveyed, less than a handful attempt to bring their readers into contact with Australian news, politics, or decisions that are directly relevant to their immediate social concerns. No doubt a few of the community's more open thinkers realise this, but they are unable to surmount the historical and religio–political forces that prove too strong for well-intentioned reformers. This has forced several Muslim communities to pay a high price. Chief among them is an unemployment figure of 28.2% (Kabir, 2006) — the highest among 160 ethnic and religious groups. Another is a recently acquired label of 'the Lebanese back', a symptom that allegedly places those claiming for Workcare benefits above any other migrant community.

An important point is that news items and editorials are written uniformly by, for and about first-generation migrants of Muslim background, with little or no attempt to cover the affairs of, or publish contributions from, the second generations. It is not, of course, merely the editorials that express a point of view, but the content of newspapers as a whole — the selection of subjects worthy of attention and the interpretation.

Rarely devoted to abstract discussions, or endorsing the benefits of integration, dialogue, and participation in the cultural, artistic and intellectual life of the Australian culture, such articles continue to dramatise the local gossip and the various intercommunity political struggles. Less than 6% of a total of 460 randomly analysed articles during a 5-year period had an 'Australian' content (please provide source of statistics with citation and reference).

Fostering a Meaningful Dialogue

The none-too-complimentary attitudes between Christian and Muslim communities continue to fill folkloric and literary pages of the two traditions. It may take a closer look to find out that interfaith couples *can* work out their religious differences, and that it is usually the families and their respective community who require a little coaxing.

In assessing the current situation, there is a need to break down stereotypes of and to remove the fear of each other's religion. Unaccommodating attitudes that take on a religious dimension can foster further misrepresentations and false interpretations.

The following affirmations, in both the Australian Muslim and Christian communities, should be fostered to promote inclusiveness, togetherness and diversity, and to dispel xenophobic attitudes:

Australian Muslim Communities

The Australian Muslim communities can play a role in bringing about various initiatives. Many ordinary and professional thinkers have become more publicly vocal. An Australian Muslim academic, Kamal Siddiqi, notes that many of the overseas resident clerics who come to Australia have little knowledge of the local culture and may inadvertently do a disservice to the community. Not only do they replace homegrown ones, but they continue to look to their home country to address local problems.

One of these would be to clarify that Muslims and Arabs cannot be lumped under one title. They may share common religious rituals and beliefs but, like the Christian communities, they are separated by denominational affiliations, language, cultural upbringing and affinities to Western cultures and political alliances. Recent research (Jupp, 2001), for example, reveals that some Australian Muslim communities share with non-Muslim communities more in their beliefs on issues of division of labour and upbringing of children than with other ethnic religious groups.

Australia's Muslim communities want to live in Australian society and not separately. Muslim thinkers are tilting in the direction of increased integration and participation in civic life. One critical step is to engage with educational curriculum consultants nationally and at a State level. They may propose the inclusion of subjects relating to their current and eventual contribution to the building of multicultural Australia, the diversity of Muslim cultures and diverse Christian (and Jewish) minorities in their countries of origin, the emerging identities of children within Christian–Muslim marriages, and their willingness to participate in the cultural, artistic, literary, and political expression of mainstream society.

They can make their position clearer about their stance on issues of extremism and moderation; that a minority of extremists do not speak in the name of a majority. In doing so, they will allay the dilemmas of many 'other' Australians in wanting to know who the moderates are and who the fanatics are. Such a dilemma was expressed in the 'Letters to the Editor' of *The Age* newspaper (2002):

> Either you are opposed to barbarism in the name of your religion or you are not ... If you do not, you shouldn't be surprised when those who are the targets of terrorists eye you suspiciously. If you are you should go on record and resist as a matter of conscience ... If you are not, you shouldn't be surprised when those who are the targets of terrorists eye you suspiciously' (p. 16).

A similar tone with a varying expression appeared in another leading paper: 'If they want to be taken seriously, instead of expressing fury over Taliban suspects being detained overnight in dog pens, Australian Muslim groups should be expressing outrage that the Taliban keep Muslim women and girls penned up permanently. Alternatively they could express outrage over the five Muslim women shot and buried alive in Pakistan for the crime of wanting to choose their own husbands. The appalling abuses of Muslim women and girls' human rights is rancid elephant in the world's kitchen (Letters to the Editor, *The Australian*, 2008).

Australian Christian Communities

The Australian Christian communities can equally play a role in rapprochement by endorsing various initiatives. Foremost of these, they can endorse the first steps of reform experienced by sections of the Muslim communities. Although their religions and cultures are different, a note underscoring that their primary motive of migrating to Australia is the safety and education of their children is in order. Their willingness to contribute to Australia is only hindered by never ending misconception, false accusations and exaggeration of difference by some sections of the broader community.

That said, significant differences in the teaching and attitudes between the two religions are not to be sidestepped due to a false sense of security. Differences of interpretation towards social values and way of life, individual accountability, consensual decision-making, and attitudes towards implementing moral imperatives do exist. It is feasible that we should be able to acknowledge them, respect them and address them without aiming at a fine compromise. Not because we no longer need a dialogue, but as Manne (2003) reasoned, because these different approaches have concrete implications to both communities living together in a shared place. He has referred to this capacity of accommodating many cultural and religious expressions within a single language, law and polity as 'multiculturalism'.

Moderate Muslims who keep their faith on a personal level, avoid politicising it, and feel embarrassed by actions made under the banner of their religion, are in particular need of such an endorsement. Absence of religious hierarchy has prompted many moderate Muslims to take matters into their own hands and become more organised. For a self-serving minority it may be politically convenient to demonise others on the basis of race or religion, but they never overcome their own phobias.

As Australian society matures into a full cultural inclusiveness, those who promote Islamophobia (Australia's fear of non-Western cultures and assertion of 'their' culture and life) shrink in numbers. When a conservative member of Parliament called for a ban on Muslim women wearing their traditional dress, he sparked an uproar both in the Parliament and community. He was made to account for his attack on the values of a religious observance and misunderstanding of the nature of religious freedom in a liberal–democratic society.

In Australian Arab Christian Communities

While the Muslim communities have had their fair share of demonisation, Christian Arabs have been treated as non-people or at best as token Christians. There is the perception that they must have converted from Islam. The code of silence has inadvertently made it politically convenient for Islaomophobes to keep the flame of hatred alive. In marginalising the Christian Arab communities they keep alive the 'Western only' Judeo-Christian agenda, and conveniently promote a sectarian anti-Muslim fanaticism that hinders steps for dialogue.

The Mainstream Versus Muslim Ethnic Media

For a long time, to be a Muslim or Arab in the Western media was to be an object of belittlement. They were made to endure the Hollywood stereotypes and religious misnomers forced on them, whether by accident or design. Unprincipled reporting has conveniently made Muslims and Arabs pay the price of the postwar guilt feelings of the Western nations.

Print and broadcast media in Australia and the United States have been selective in foreign news coverage, leading to a poorly educated Australian public. This may be one of the reasons that some Australians, and most Americans, were so shocked by the events of September 11 — they have little or no knowledge of politics, ideology or religion in the rest of the world. Yet the space given to crime, violence, sex, and scandals has greatly increased.

In the same vein, the Muslim community plays a part in formulating the reactions of the main society. The dozen or so ethnic Arab Muslim papers have been a channel through which the community vents its own political and cultural frustrations, although at a price. Among its failings, the Muslim–Arabic press, despite the proclaimed good intentions of some editors, tends to accentuate the political and socioeconomic divisions between the various sections of the community. It devotes some 85% of its space to the ethnic community and news of the home country of origin, with only a portion devoted to Australian society.

The Muslim–Arabic press has succeeded in perpetuating a native cultural tradition in a host society, perhaps more so than any other migrant press. With time this isolation may give way to strengthening integration. It may provide the community with increased confidence and sufficient bonding to enable bicultural values.

The flow of information and a sense of fair play is a two-way process. While the ethnic Muslim communities and their press have been less sophisticated and more cut off from the mainstream cultural life, today more second-generation migrants writing and editing in the mainstream media will speed up the process of integration and mutual respect.

Ultimately each community should ask: What are we doing to portray a better image of the other community?

Author's Note

A modified version of this chapter appeared in Daverth, J. (Ed.) *Conflict and Conciliation,* Columba Press, 2007.

References

Ata, A. (1980). *Acculturation of Lebanese Christians and Muslims in Australia.* Unpublished PhD thesis, University of Melbourne, Australia.
Ata, A., & Batrouney, T. (1989). Attitudes and stereotyping in Victorian secondary schools. *The Eastern Anthropologist, 42*(1), 35–50.
Bloul, R. (2002). Being Muslim in the West: The case of Australian Muslims. *Australian Review Public Affairs,* Digest 15, 1.
Bone, P. (2002, July 24). Rape: The debate we have to have. *The Age,* p. 15.
Jupp, J. (Ed.) 2001. *The encyclopaedia of the Australian people.* Canberra, Australia: AGPS.
Kabir, N. (2002). Depiction of Muslims in selected Australian media. *Media and Culture Journal, 9*(4), 1–4.
King, J. (2002, June 5). There is no Yes but …, in 'Letters and Opinion'. *The Age,* p. 16.
Letters to the editor. (2002, June 5). *The Age,* p. 14.
Letters to the editor. (2002, October 23). *The Age,* p. 16.
Letters to the editor. (2008, September 3). *The Australian,* p. 13.
Manne, R. (2003, August 25). West is best: The faulty heart of Islamophobia. *The Age,* p. 17.
Miles, J. (2002). Theology and clash of civilisations. *Cross Currents, 51*(4), 4.
Shirley, K. (1970). The Arab world. In *Oxford Childrens Reference Library* (p. 10.). Oxford: Oxford University Press.

Chapter 2

Christian–Muslim Households
Identity and Attitudes to Their 'Australian' Children

Perspectives on Religious and Cultural Identification

Intermarriage, being the most committed and intimate of relationships, is perhaps one of the finest predictors about the presence or absence of prejudice between members of the host and minority communities. This suggests that interfaith dialogue and tolerance are an integral part of the two communities, as reflected within interfaith families. It may also mean that guardians of the ethnic or minority traditions have lost hold on their members and, in particular, those from the first generation in relation to members of the second generation (Birrell & Healy, 2000).

One of the struggles interfaith couples face is how they can remain respectful towards their own religious and cultural preferences, given the pressures of their children's identity and those from their extended family. Even after they have sorted out differences between themselves, those who have decided to have children will find, to their surprise (or disappointment), that cultural attitudes that may have been dormant have surfaced with the arrival of their children. In addition to ongoing discussions about care and discipline, parents must also renegotiate rearing practices, social and religious behaviour, and conform to what schools dictate, relations with in-laws, and maintaining non-Anglo names.

Although these issues may drive a wedge between interreligious or intercultural married couples, they may also have the potential to enhance their relationship with a stronger bond, one that provides deeper and more meaningful insights. Researchers on mixed marriages caution that the greatest danger lies in raising children within a particular cultural background, and blaming a partner's culture for the inevitable conflicts that emerge (Penny & Khoo, 1996).

What determines the impact on the children of two religions is linked to several factors. First is the extent of loyalty of each of the parents to what the community believes; for example, how tolerant are they in having the children speak the language of one or other of the parents, how sensitive is the culture of the parents to the independence of the children, and what kind of interaction is there between the community and parents (Penny & Khoo, 1996).

While this is relatively easy for inter-Christian couples (Ata, 2002), striking a workable balance can be elusive. Those children who try to be respectful to both spouses' traditions can find that it harms their efforts to bond with one of the traditions to which they may be attracted, eventually causing a negative impact on their own sense of identity. However, in the majority of cases, the desire of parents to have children respect both faith traditions, and to acquire an independently and healthy religious identity, is not mutually exclusive.

Some chose an ecumenical escape route, particularly in abstaining from attending public worship. Those who endeavoured to respond to only one spouse's religious and cultural preferences came to have feelings of instability (Penny & Khoo study, 1996; Ata, 2002).

Methodology

A sample size of 106 people formed the basis of analysis (Ata, 2002). They were selected from Victoria, with the majority being residents of Melbourne. The sample size, although considered small for a comprehensive study, was examined over a period of several months. A total of 11 families declined to be interviewed. Two sets of questionnaires where given to participants — Christian and Muslim husbands and wives: (1) a comprehensive questionnaire where their responses will be referred to as 'Self' in accompanying tables; (2) a minor questionnaire that pertains to the spouses who were not available at the time of the survey. These are referred to throughout this article as 'partners or spouses'. Where there are no bars for partners or spouses in a specific table it is because they were not given the full questionnaire.

Table 2.1
Sex and Religion of Participants Before Marriage

	Males	Females
Muslim	44	33
Christian	19	10
Total	63	43

Table 2.2
Religion Before and After Marriage

Religion	Self		Partner	
	Before	After	Before	After
Muslim	73%	81%	26%	35%
Christian	27%	19%	74%	65%

Findings in this chapter are largely derived from a major survey titled 'Christian Muslims Intermarriage in Australia', and published as a book by David Lovell Publishing in 2003.

There were 44 Muslim and 19 Christian male participants, and 33 Muslim and 10 Christian female participants, of which 28% were born in Australia (Table 2.1). The remainder were born in Europe (48%), Asia (15%) and the Middle East.

A sizable group (48%) indicated that they had fully or partly completed their tertiary education.

Other demographic data reveal that 85% have obtained Australian citizenship; the remainder are either migrants or have decided not to initiate a request for naturalisation. Of the former group, 72% were born in Australia compared with 58% of their partners. The remainder cited Europe (mainly Eastern Europe), non-Muslim Asia, the Middle East, and other Muslim countries including Pakistan and Malaysia as their place of birth. Of the total number of participants 43% were native English speakers.

The shift of the Christian partners into affiliating with their Muslim spouse is clearly evident. When the gender breakdown factor is introduced, one notices a greater shift among the Christian female spouses toward the Muslim faith (Table 2.2). Identifying with either religion after marriage, even though half of the participants reported choosing civil marriages, is a factor that will be clarified elsewhere.

A few couples were hesitant about discussing their partner's assumptions or feelings about choosing a religious or non-religious name, school, religious affiliation, baptism, cultural identity, and so on, as they felt that such discussions might interfere with the fabric of a developing relationship.

Discussion of Findings

It is encouraging to note that a majority of families (45%) allow their children, or will do so in the future, to choose their own religion, and only 17% object to this (Table 2.3).

Table 2.3
Attitudes of Parents to Children's Choice of Religion

	Yes	No	Don't know
Q: 'Do you object if your children choose their own religion?'	17%	45%	32%
Q: 'Will you give your children the freedom to marry a partner from a different religion?'	60%	15%	19%

It is common that interfaith parents acquire a broader knowledge and appreciation of other religions as they watch their children develop their own. When parents mutually agree to pass on training and advice that is consistent with their faiths, they perceive their household as harmonious. Such parents encourage their children to show equal respect to the two traditions, as they are being raised in two traditions. They hope that any confusion will be minimal and that whenever contradictions are perceived they will be tolerated and not denigrated. They hope they will not feel that there is anything wrong or bad if their children decide to follow some other faith in the future.

With regard to allowing children to marry a partner from a different religion, as we have noted earlier, the 'Yes' vote is high (60%). This can in part be explained by the fact that the Muslim community allows its members to marry people from other religions, with the proviso that only males are sanctioned to make such an alliance.

Support for these observations is detailed in subsequent findings (Ata, 2005) in response to the questions listed in Table 2.4. These findings show that in real-life situations, thinking and practice are on the way to merging. They show that it is possible for couples to effectively negotiate religious differences, and that problems are not insurmountable. These couples deny that

Table 2.4
Responses to Questions on Children's Religious and Moral Upbringing

	Self	Partner	Both
Q: 'Who is (will be) mostly in charge of the religious upbringing of your children?'	25%	11%	52%
Q: 'Who is (will be) mostly in charge of rearing your children?'	0%	8%	64%
Q: 'What religion would you want your children to follow?'	43%	0%	48%

their move to enter into interfaith marriage is a liability that may compromise their children's spiritual or social standing. A fair number of participants who felt this way stressed that they did not wish to interfere with the religious choices made by their children.

As shown in Table 2.3, 60% were agreeable to permitting their children to choose their own religion. However, this is slightly at odds with the response to the question in Table 2.4, where 43% indicated that they would want their children to follow their own religion. This group is almost equal to those who prefer that their children follow the religious tradition of both partners.

Parental expectations

The majority of couples interviewed had children. Only 18 families, or 16%, did not have any children. Almost half (48.2%) had one or two children, and 27.7% had three. The mean number of children per family in the survey sample was 2.6.

It is possible that the demography has changed because in Western cultures education is a strong factor in a lower birth rate. As rearing children becomes more valued in a fragmenting world, so more attention and care is given to fewer children. The deterioration of the environment and climate change can also influence parents to choose to have fewer children.

These new realities of differing needs and forms of family structure are currently producing different governmental policies. The traditional idea of a two-parent family is changing, with many new social services supporting single-parent families. For example, the latest Australian census (Australian Bureau of Statistics, 2006) showed that 40% of the population live in households on their own. It is interesting to speculate how far away mixed marriage couples are from producing these kinds of figures.

Figure 2.1 shows the types of schools to which parents of mixed marriages send their children. It is interesting to note that while 71.4% of children attended school, only 13% attended Muslim schools. This figure is comparatively small, given that almost 71% of the spouses were Muslim-born.

Those who selected government schools, which are secular in nature, comprised 58% of the total, while the remainder (17%) preferred Christian or independent schools.

It is difficult to predict future trends in schooling; 20.3% were too young to attend and 8.3% did not have children.

Attitudes underlying parental decisions are predicated on their beliefs about whether their children benefit or suffer because they come from a mixed marriage. Variations in such beliefs surface when introducing variables relating to birth, sex, and previous religion of the spouses (Figure 2.2).

Question: 'What kind of school do you/will you send your children to?'

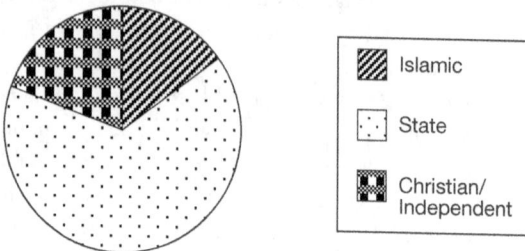

Figure 2.1
Types of schools to which participants of mixed marriages send/will send their children.

Many reasons were provided for the viewpoints expressed on this subject, which emanated from differing philosophies, personal dispositions and feelings. A selection of these is quoted below (Ata, 2005):

> It all depends on the parents, it could be an enriching experience or cause suffering. But when they are subject to two religions it gives you a chance to learn about both and become more tolerant and accepting to other religions.
>
> My [Muslim] husband is dark-skinned, I am white [Catholic-born Muslim convert] — and our children know this is a special marriage.
>
> They will be more aware of the differences of the world. Enriched. They learn two cultures, values, and traditions. The trade-off is there will be some suffering. The world is narrow-minded, and communities do

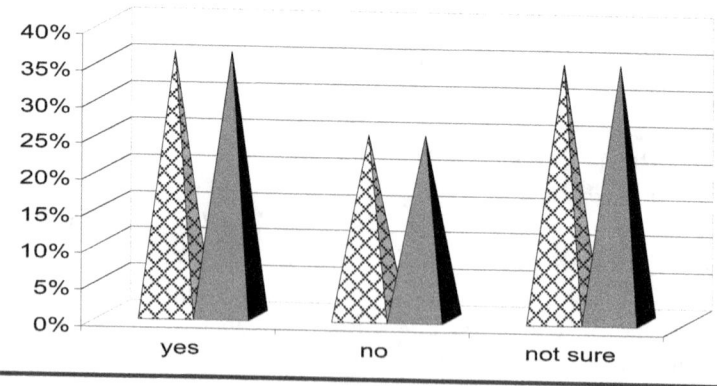

Figure 2.2
Spouses' prediction of children benefitting because of parental mixed marriage.

ostracise children and families. Mostly 'Yes' with irregularity depending on class background and upbringing.

Difficult to say. Our children grew up OK in a stable home. Can't say if it was a benefit. Maybe because religion was not a factor in our home.

No, I do not think they benefit. I think it confuses them. Yes, I do think they suffer. All their lives they get different messages from their parents. They will not be confident even with a false sense of it. It is confusing, isn't it!

The findings shown in Figure 2.3 illustrate what this study set out to discover in terms of possible changing religious and cultural trends and in terms of the societal reactions and adaptability of second generation children.

One-fifth of the population (20.5%) is adamant about not wanting their children to affiliate with either Muslim or Christian communities. A female Christian academic made the following remarks:

They [the neighbour's children] already call him [her son] Ibn il-Masihiyyeh [the son of the Christian mother]. How can you be oblivious to the stares and audible whispers? If it were in the United States between blacks and whites you will understand that. But we are here not there.

The question is, to what extent must attitudinal change impact on the community and its leadership in order for them to tolerate a public announcement of this sort, given the traditional legal consequences of such proclamations?

Depending on one's predetermined leanings, 45% advocating a religious choice would constitute a nucleus for change, together with the former group. The remainder (28.6%) seem to have made up their minds: their children must follow their religion. Of those who expressed this attitude, 84% were Muslim affiliates.

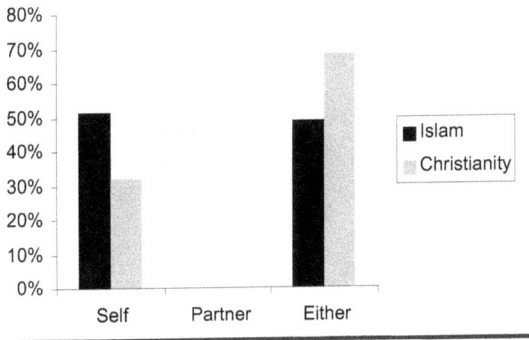

Figure 2.3
Reponses to the question 'What religion would you like your children to follow?' by religion.

Almost twice the proportion of Muslims participants (49.5%) agreed that their children may follow either religion. Of the Christians, 32% would prefer their children to follow their own religion instead of their partner's, while the majority (68%) would allow their children to follow either religion. The difference on this variable is significant and contrasts with the gender variable in which the preference was equally distributed. In the case of gender, approximately 48% of both sexes preferred their children to follow their own religion compared with 52% indicating either religion.

When the birthplace factor was introduced, the ratio of European-born (56%) was significantly higher than the Australian- (42%) or Middle-Eastern-born (42%) in expecting their children to only follow their own religion.

To validate the participants' attitudes analysed earlier, the question of the children's religion was introduced from the following angle: 'Would you object if your children chose their own religion?' (Figures 2.4–2.6).

These findings clearly show that differences in attitudes exist between Muslims and Christians, males and females, as well as European- and Australian-born participants. Using religion as an indicator showed 75% of Christians and 39% of Muslims do not object to their children choosing their own religion.

Of the female participants 63%, compared with 37% of males, gave a similar response. Of the European-born, 33% gave such a response compared with 53% Middle-Easterners and 62% of the Australian-born. In order to make a generalised statement as to whether participants who are Christian, females, and Australian-born have a more liberal attitude with regards to their children a range of other variables have to be integrated.

Having made up their minds about the religious choice for their children, parental expectations of the kind of life that their children will lead were

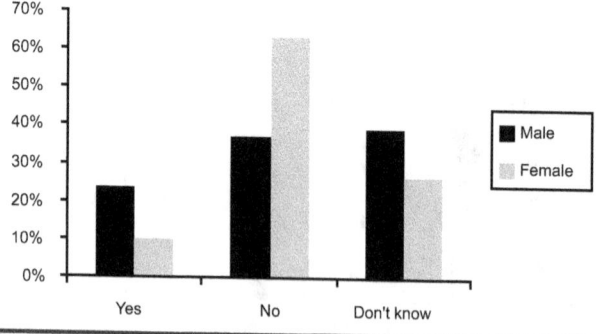

Figure 2.4
Responses to the question: 'Would you object if your children chose their own religion?' by gender of participants.

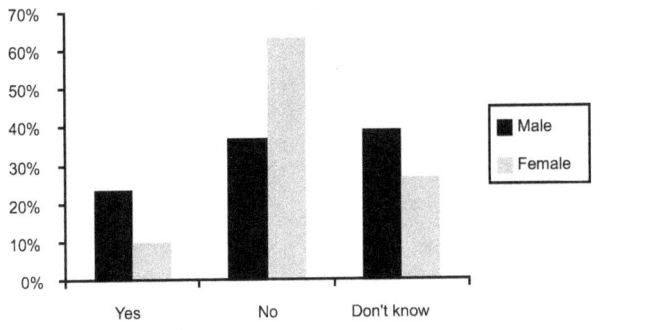

Figure 2.5
Responses to the question: 'Would you object if your children chose their own religion?' by religion of participants.

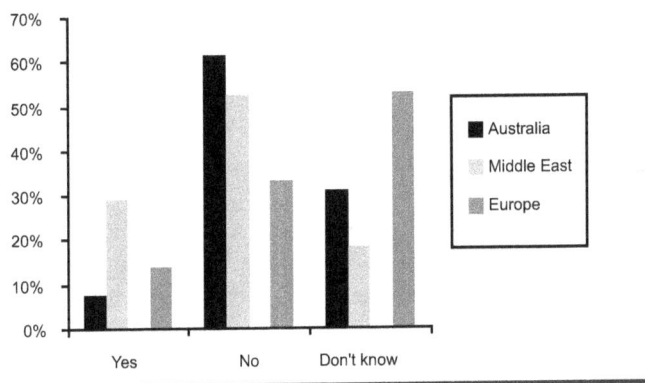

Figure 2.6
Responses to the question: 'Would you object if your children chose their own religion?' by place of birth.

expressed in Figures 2.7 to 2.9. The largest group (52.7%) believed that the lifestyle of their children will be 'better', contrasted with 5.4% indicating 'worse' and 9.8% 'the same'. Still, one-third (31.3%) are not certain about this matter.

Not being able to predict how their children will be perceived in the future was problematic. In circumstances where religion and state function separately, as in many Western societies, the 'do not know' response may signify a sense of discomfort about their children's future, although not primarily about their religious sense of belonging, but rather the lack of it.

Christian spouses who were uneasy about their children not being baptised felt that this might determine the direction and place of worship for the family as a whole in the future. Clearly, this group is more inclined to reflect atti-

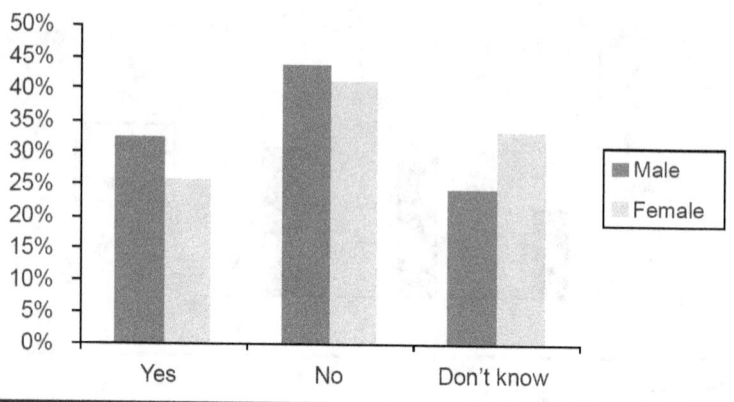

Figure 2.7
Responses to the question: 'Do you think that children will suffer because they come from a mixed marriage' by gender.

tudes not subjected to conditioning, and show a similar leaning with regards to not being certain whether their children will suffer from a mixed marriage.

These children can develop a healthy self-belief and are better able to deal with discrimination from the outside, without losing self-confidence and self-worth (Romano, 1988).

Findings related to variables that have a bearing on who is responsible for the religious upbringing of the children, such as religion, gender and place of birth, were explored. With regard to religion, the overwhelming majority of

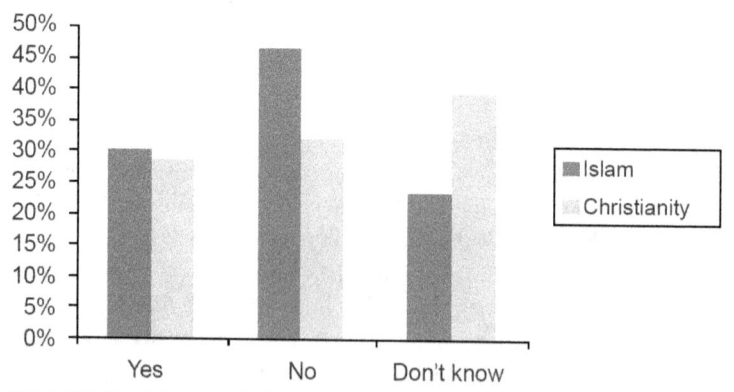

Figure 2.8
Responses to the question: 'Do you think that children will suffer because they come from a mixed marriage' by religion.

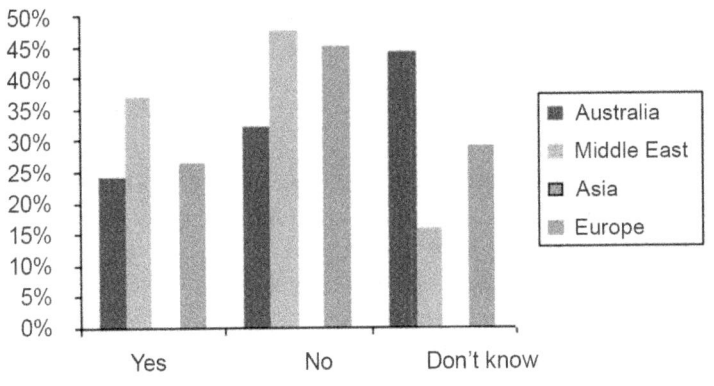

Figure 2.9
Responses to the question: 'Do you think that children will suffer because they come from a mixed marriage?' by place of birth of participants.

Christians (86%) indicated that either spouse is in charge of the religious upbringing of their children. In other words, the responsibility is shared.

By comparison, 50% of Muslims shared the role and 33% advocated themselves as being solely in charge of that aspect of their children's lives. The comparison of responses between the two groups is significant, foreshadowing several other variables, including the level of education and the frequency of attendance or involvement in one's religious institution. No significant variation was found in the remaining factors of gender and place of birth.

Data from a follow-up study about intermarriage between Catholic and other Christian Australians was not available for the purposes of comparison (Ata, 2005). The current data is in itself promising when one refers to a shared responsibility in this area.

It could be that uncertainty about whether the children would fit into an ever-changing multicultural society has influenced the upholding of the patriarchal role of the husband, perhaps as a psychological and practical reaction against the perceived threat against community life.

Conclusions

Mixed marriages in Australian society have brought with them mixed outcomes. At one level, couples in such marriages are far from being fully integrated into the mainstream society. The findings show that significance and contrasting differences do exist between Christians and Muslims, males and females, as well as European — and Australian-born participants. They reveal that 75% Christian born compared with 39% Muslim-born spouses; 63%

females compared with 37% males; and 33% European born compared with 53% Middle-Eastern born and 62% Australian born do not object to their children choosing their own religion. There is currently little indication as to whether their children will make headway as time passes. Clearly, without major adjustment by the community at large to this newly emerging paradigm of partnership, Christian–Muslim marriages are doomed to failure. The premise underlying this is that although the two religions may overlap in many extraordinary ways, many of their principles are not compatible.

On another level there are signs that such couples have been enriched and diversified in their outlook and relationship. A dual awareness was clearly shown from all who were interviewed. Despite the relative diversity of reactions, a large proportion of Muslim spouses state that they still cherish taking part in a mixed marriage, as long as it is practised within an overall Islamic sphere. The ratio of Muslim spouses (40.9%) to Christians (16%) opposing their children choosing their religion was three to one — a response forming a nucleus for a positive change.

Those who believed that the lifestyle of their children would be 'better' in the future (52.7%) constituted a majority. By contrast, 5.4% indicated 'worse', 9.8% indicated 'the same', and one-third (31.3%) were not so sure.

These results may be viewed as the seeds of change from the way previous generations from particular religious–ethnic backgrounds used to identify themselves. It may be that this group signals a departure from accepting that nationality and religious affiliation are one and the same. The two ingredients may be viewed as synonymous only insofar as couples of mixed marriages view their sense of destiny as identical.

Finding common ground between Christians and Muslims can only be of benefit to future generations. The effect of interreligious intermarriage extends beyond the confines of a relationship between two individuals and can help find that common ground within the greater community. This will also allay insecurity and fear, and diminish the power struggle that may exist between religions.

Reference

Penny, J., & Khoo, S.-E. (1996). *Intermarriage: A study of migration and integration*. Canberra, Australia: Australian Government Printing Service.

Bibliography

Adams, B. (1986). *The family: A sociological interpretation*. New York: Harcourt, Brace Jovanovich.

Al-Haj, M. (1983). *Family lifestyles in an Arab town in Israel*. Unpublished doctoral dissertation, Hebrew University, Jerusalem.

Al-Haj, M. (1988). The changing Arab kinship structure: The effect of modernization in an urban community. *Economic Development and Cultural Change, 36*(2), 237–258.

Ata, A.W. (1980a). The Lebanese community in Melbourne: Ethnicity and acculturation. Unpublished doctoral dissertation, University of Melbourne, Melbourne, Australia.

Ata, A.W. (1980b). Marriage patterns among the Lebanese community in Melbourne. *Australian and New Zealand Journal of Sociology, 16*(3), 112–113.

Ata, A.W. (1981). Prospects and retrospects on the role of Muslim Arab women at present: trends and tendencies. *Islamic Culture, 55*(4), 259–276.

Ata, A.W. (1984). Impact of westernization, and other forces, on the status of Muslim women in the Arab Middle East. *The Eastern Anthropologist, 37*(2), 95–126.

Ata, A.W. (1986). *The West Bank Palestinian family*. London: Kegan Paul International

Ata, A.W. (1988–1990). *Religion and ethnic identity*. (Vols. 1–3). Melbourne, Australia: Spectrum Publications.

Ata, A.W. (1994). *Bereavement and health: Gender, religious, psychological and cross-cultural issues*. Melbourne: David Lovell Publishing.

Ata, A.W. (2000). *Intermarriage between Christians and Muslims: A West Bank study*. Melbourne, Australia: David Lovell Publishing.

Ata, A.W. (2002). *Christian Muslim intermarriage in Australia: Social cohesion or cultural fragmentation*. Melbourne, Australia: David Lovell Publishing.

Ata, A.W. (2005). *Mixed marriages: Catholic/Non-Catholic marriages in Australia*. Melbourne, Australia: David Lovell Publishing.

Ateeq, N., Duaybis, C., & Schrader, M. (1997). *Jerusalem: What makes for peace?* London: Milesende.

Avruch, K., & Black, P. (1993). Conflict resolution in inter-cultural settings: Problems and prospects. In D. Sandole, & H. Van der Merwe (Eds.), *Conflict resolution theory and practice: Integration and application.*. New York: St Martin's Press.

Bajeva, M. (1981). *Women in Islam*. New York: Advent Books.

Beck, U. (1999). *World risk society*. Cambridge: Polity Press.

Betts, R. (1978). *Christians in the Arab east*. Atlanta: John Knox Press.

Birrell, B. (1995). Spouse migration to Australia. *People and Place, 3*(1), 9–16.

Birrell, B., & Healy, E. (2000). Out-marriage and the survival of ethnic communities in Australia. *People and Place, 8*(3), 37–46.

Blau, P., Blum, T., & Schwartz, J. (1982). Heterogeneity and intermarriage. *American Sociological Review, 47*, 45–62.

Bouma, G. (1994). *Mosques and Muslim settlement in Australia*. Canberra, Australia: AGPS.

Esposito, J. (1997). Christian-Muslim relations in historic perspective. In N. Ateeq, C. Duaybis, & M. Schrader (Eds.), *Jerusalem: What makes for peace?* (pp. 31–37). London: Milesende.

Esposito, J. (1999). *The Islamic threat: Myth or reality?* (3rd ed.). New York: Oxford University Press.

Gariano, A. (1994). Religious identification and marriage. *People and Place, 2*(1), 41–47.

Gariano, A., & Rutland, D. (1997). Religious intermix: 1996 census update. *People and Place, 5*(4), 14.

Goodnow, J. & Cashmore, J. (1985). Parents expectations in some Australian groups: Cultural differences. In M. Poole & B. Randhawa (Eds.), *Australia in transition: Culture and life possibilities* (pp. 233–244). Sydney, Australia: Harcourt, Brace Jovanovich.

Gray, A. (1987). Intermarriage, opportunity and preference. *Population Studies, 41*, 365–379.

Gray, A. (1989). Measuring preference in intermarriage: A response to McCaa. *Population Studies, 43*(1), 163–166.

Hanson, V. (2002). Why the Muslims misjudged us. *City Journal, 12*(1), 8.

Penny, J., & Khoo, S.-E. (1996). *Intermarriage: A study of migration and integration.* Canberra, Australia: Australian Government Printing Service.

Price, C. (1988–1989). The melting pot is working. *IPA Review, 2*(3), 34–35.

Price, C. (1994). Ethnic intermixture in Australia. *People and Place, 2*(4), 8–11.

Price, C., & Zubrzycki, J. (1962). The use of intermarriage statistics as an index of intermarriage. *Population Studies, 15*, 58–69.

Prior, M., & Taylor, W. (Eds). (1994). *Christians in the holy land.* London: The World of Islam Trust.

Quandagno, J. (1981). The Italian American Family. In C. Mindel, R. Habestein & R.Wright (Eds.). *Ethnic families in America: Patterns and variations* (pp. 61–85). New York: Elsevier.

Raheb, M. (1995). *I am a Palestinian Christian.* Minneapolis: Fortress Press.

Romano, D. (1988). *Intercultural marriage: Promises and pitfalls.* Yarmouth, MA: Intercultural Press.

Stephan, C and Stephan, W. (1989). After intermarriage: Ethnic identity among mixed-heritage. *Journal of Marriage and Family, 51*(2), 507–551.

Stevens, G. (1985). Nativity, intermarriage and mother tongue shift. *American Sociological Review, 50*, 74–83.

Smart, N. (1966). Global Christian theology and education. In J. Astley & L. Francis (Eds.), *Christian theology and religious education: Connections and contradictions* (pp. 7–15). London: Society for Promoting Christian Knowledge (SPCK).

Storer, D. (1995). *Ethnic family values in Australia.* Sydney, Australia: Prentice Hall.

Chapter 3

Attitudes of School-Age Non-Muslim Australians Towards Muslims and Islam:
A National Survey

The Muslim community, although small, is one of the fastest growing religious communities in Australia, but has been little studied by researchers. Media interest and government press releases about stereotyping of Muslim communities has come into focus during the last decade.

To a certain degree the media image of how Muslim communities portray a threat to the mainstream civic Australian life may have worked its way into the consciousness of Muslim and non-Muslim students alike.

This chapter reports some results from a large-scale study of attitudes towards Islam and Muslims among Australian secondary students. Widespread negative stereotypes, and the relatively new presence of the Muslim community in Australia, tend to suggest non-Muslim students may not be well informed, while the longstanding multicultural posture of educational policy suggests otherwise. Variations in responses between boys and girls, and religious or non-religious affiliated students were apparent. The findings show Australian students are generally ignorant about Muslims and Islam, and few believe that schools are filling the gaps in their knowledge. While non-Muslim students agree that acceptance of Muslims does not come easily in Australia, school does not emerge as a site for change.

Methods
Participants
The participants were 1,000 students enrolled at 20 secondary schools from around Australia (excluding the Northern Territory and Western Australia[1])

who were administered a full-length survey examining general attitudes towards Muslims and Islam. Participating students were from Years 10–12.[2]

Secondary schools of Muslim or Jewish affiliation were not approached for this survey, nor were Muslim or Jewish students. It is anticipated that differences will exist within these groups towards Muslims and Islam, and it is intended to examine these groups in subsequent surveys. However, the responses of Muslim and Jewish students are likely to be unrepresentative of most Australians. The particular characteristics of our sample are presented in Table 3.1.

The sample consisted of 43% boys and 57% girls. Most respondents (42%) were at schools in New South Wales (NSW) and the Australian Capital Territory (ACT), about a third (34%) were from Victoria, and the rest were from Queensland (5%), South Australia (8%) and Tasmania (11%).

About half the sample came from Catholic schools (53%), and roughly one-quarter each were from other Christian schools (26%) and non-denominational schools (21%). Most students (92%) were born in Australia, and 81% spoke only English at home. Few respondents (7%) had any Muslim neighbours.

Over half the respondents were at coeducational schools (58%), a minority at boys-only schools (14%), and about a quarter at girls-only schools (28%).

In total, 14 demographic attributes were recorded for each respondent, 10 relating to the respondent and four to the respondent's school.

Table 3.1[3]
Participant Characteristics by Gender (N = 1000)*

	Female (n = 655)	Male (n = 340)	Total
Language			
English only	518	289	807
Other: English and Other	136	50	186
Religion			
Christian	490	259	749
Non-religious	152	74	226
Personal social distance to other race	2.10 (0.9)	2.48 (1.0)**	2.23 (0.9)
Perceived parental social distance to other race	2.19 (1.0)	2.34 (0.9)**	2.25 (0.9)
Personal social distance to Muslims	2.86 (1.0)	3.20 (1.0)**	2.98 (0.9)
Perceived parental social distance to Muslims	2.82 (1.0)	2.94 (1.0)	2.86 (1.0)

Table 3.1 continued
Participant Characteristics by Gender (N = 1000)*

	Female (n = 655)	Male (n = 340)	Total
Do you have Muslim friends?			
Yes	171	45	216
No	482	293	775
Do you have Muslim neighbours?			
Yes	43	11	54
No	612	329	941
Knowledge of Islam	2.88 (2.4)	3.34 (2.5)**	3.03 (2.4)
Attitude of school education about Muslims	3.51 (1.0)	3.49 (1.0)	3.51 (1.0)
Location			
Metropolitan	256	46	302
Non-metropolitan	399	294	693
School type			
Private	569	311	880
State	86	29	115
School type			
Coeducational	385	320	705
Girls only	270	0	270
Boys only	0	20	20
Year level			
10	21	11	33
11	329	219	548
12	295	107	402
State			
NSW and ACT	292	181	473
Vic.	119	82	201
Qld	31	0	31
SA	90	18	108
Tas.	123	59	182

Note: * $p < .05$ for gender comparison
 ** $p < .01$ for gender comparison

Results

Under each heading we first present results relating to the sample as a whole. Although the survey sample was not selected in a formally random way, it was large and was drawn from a wide geographic range of schools. Hence, we believe it is likely to be quite representative of secondary students in Australia.

Three open-ended questions were put to respondents and the answers coded into a manageable number of categories as shown below. Naturally this entailed a degree of subjective judgment.

What are the first words that come into your mind when the word 'Muslim' is mentioned?

When asked the first words that come [to] mind when the word 'Muslim' is mentioned, respondents overwhelmingly (82%) offered either negative comments or comments that alluded to the differences between them and Muslims (Figure 3.1). Only 7% mentioned anything unequivocally positive. Of the 28% offering negative comments, 20% mentioned terrorism (half of them in combination with another comment) and the rest (8%) gave some other negative comment. Of the 54% alluding to differences, 13% stressed the appearance of Muslims. About one respondent in eight (12%) gave no response.

What do you like most about Muslims?

When asked what they liked most about Muslims, just under two-thirds offered a comment of some kind (Figure 3.2). Forty-four per cent gave positive comments: 4% alluded to courage, often with a mention of the difficult time Muslims have in Australia; 10% saw Muslims as benign just like other Australians; and 30% gave other positive comments. Seventeen per cent of respondents gave superficial or facetious comments (7%), or explicitly stated that they could not think of anything they 'liked most about Muslims' (this is not to be confused with non-response, which might signify simply lack of motivation to respond). Just over a third of respondents (37%) gave no response.

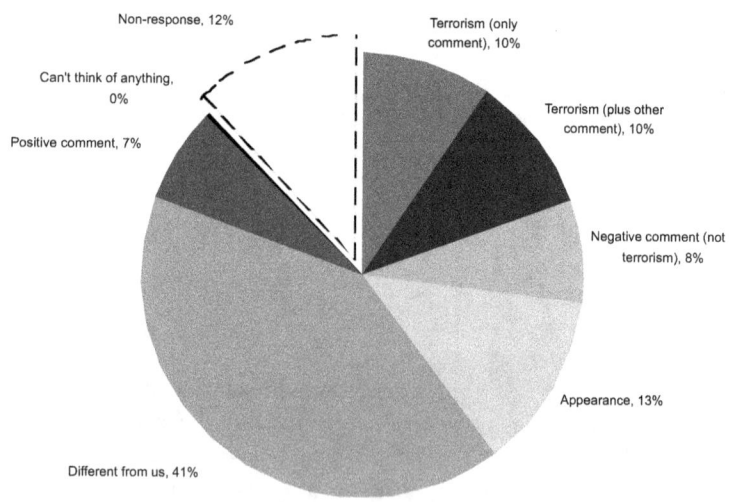

Figure 3.1
Response to 'What are the first words that come into your mind when the word 'Muslim' is mentioned?'
Note: Apparent errors in addition are due to rounding. N = 2023 (inc. non-response)

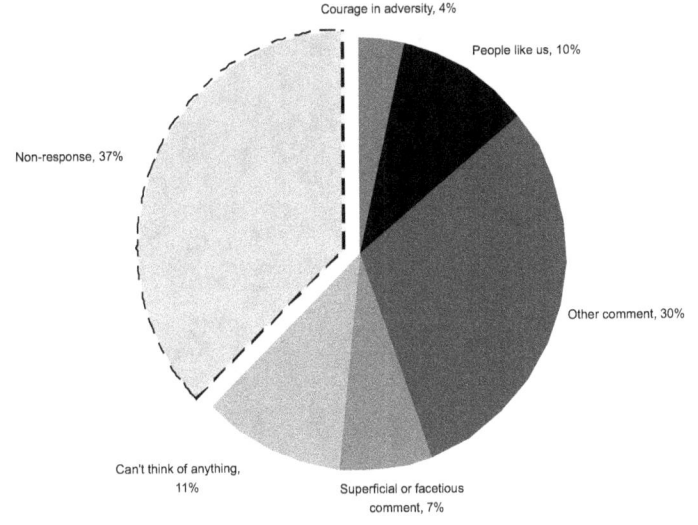

Figure 3.2
Response to 'What do you like most about Muslims?'

What do you like least about Muslims?
When asked what they liked least about Muslims, just under two-thirds offered a comment of some kind (Figure 3.3). Twenty-seven per cent mentioned terrorism, 8% alluded to the poor media image of Muslims, 5% alluded to threats to the Australian way of life, and 9% stressed the strangeness of Muslims. Seven per cent of respondents gave ambivalent comments of some kind, and 9% explicitly stated that they could not think of anything they 'liked least about Muslims' (not to be confused with a non-response, which might signify simply lack of motivation to respond). Just over a third of respondents (38%) gave no response.

Do Australians have good feelings about Muslims?
Goodwill towards the Muslim community resonates with more participants than otherwise. There are twice as many respondents (35% + 7% contrasted with 19% + 2%) who believe that most Australians have good feelings for Muslims (Figure 3.4). As a result it is correct to conclude that they are perceived as been accepted in the wider mainstream society. Those who expressed neutrality (38%) may want to seek firmer evidence of this reality.

Having characterised the entire sample, we next compare subgroups within the sample to address the question, do particular groups of respondents systematically differ in their attitudes towards Muslims and, if so, how? This

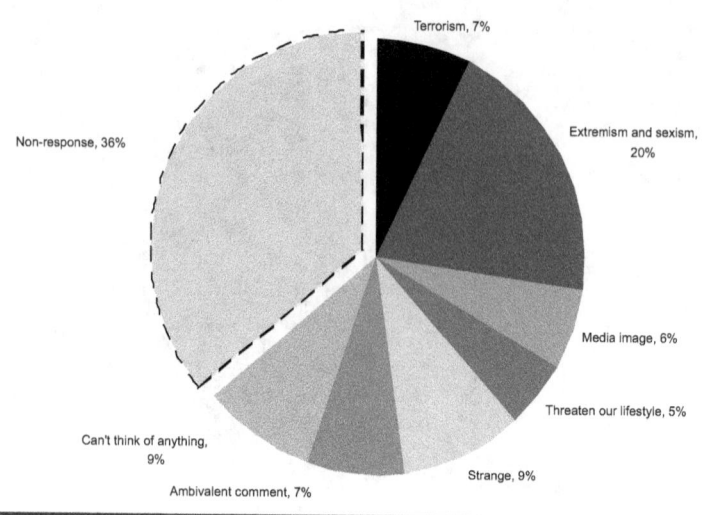

Figure 3.3
Response to 'What do you like least about Muslims?'

is of interest because it shows where and to whom policy measures might be directed.

How students differ in their attitudes

Religion played a significant role in this area. There was a strong tendency for the two Christian groups (Catholics and Other Christians) to be less well-disposed towards Muslims and Islam than were the non-religious. On two statements, all three religious affiliations differed significantly from each other.

With respect to the statement, 'Muslims threaten the Australian way of life', all disagreed, but to different degrees: Non-religious students disagreed most, followed by Catholics, and Other Christians disagreed least.

All agreed with the statement, 'Most Muslims treat women with less respect than do other Australians'; Other Christians agreed most, Catholics next, Non-religious least.

On one statement, 'Australian TV and newspapers show Muslims in a fair way', all disagreed. Other Christians and Non-religious did not differ significantly, but did differ from Catholics who disagreed least.

Regarding gender differences, boys were less accepting of Muslims and Islam than were girls. Interestingly, boys agreed more than girls with the statement, 'Most Muslims treat women with less respect than do other Australians'. This view is clearly not based on direct experience.

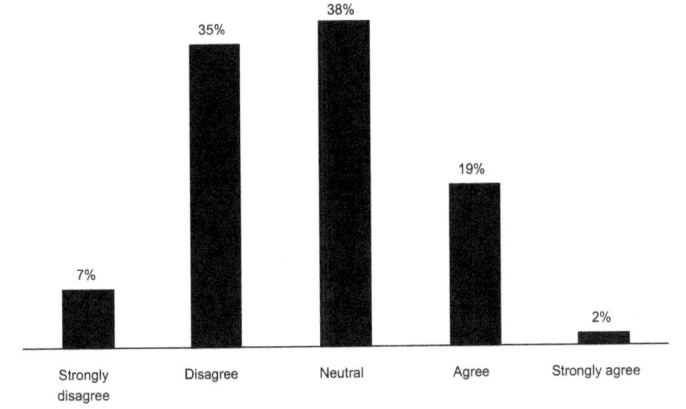

Figure 3.4
Proportion of respondents to the statement 'Most Australians have good feelings for Muslims'.

Significant differences were found between the responses of boys and girls to a number of statements. These are listed in Table 3.2.

Does having Muslim friends make a difference? In a word, yes. Significant differences were found between the responses of those with Muslim friends and those without (Table 3.3).

These findings suggest that those with Muslim friends tend to endorse positive attitudes towards Muslims, and although those who lack Muslim friends do not always endorse negative attitudes, they do tend to disagree less with them. In other words, positive attitudes are generally embraced by both groups, but more strongly by those with Muslim friends, and negative attitudes are generally opposed by both groups, but more strongly by those with Muslim friends.

Note that these findings say nothing about causation. Having Muslim friends might give rise to positive attitudes, or alternatively having positive attitudes might predispose one to seek or accept Muslim friends. Nevertheless, the two are strongly associated in a statistical sense, meaning that if one is present, the other is likely to be also.

State school students felt more positively (less negatively) about Muslims and Islam than did private school students. Of particular interest, State school students endorsed the statement, 'Australian schools should teach more about Muslims', whereas private school students did not.

We cannot say that contact with Muslims reduces prejudice, merely that it is associated with reduced prejudice. It may be that people with reduced prejudice seek out Muslim friends. This issue would need to be disentangled with longitudinal analyses if we are to discover causality, although we suggest that the

Table 3.2
Gender Differences in Responses to Select Attitudinal Statements

Boys agreed more, or disagreed less, than girls	Girls agreed more, or disagreed less, than boys
• Most Muslims treat women with less respect than do other Australians. • Muslims threaten the Australian way of life. • Most religious fanatics these days are Muslims. • Most migrants are racist. • Most Australians are racist. • Australian TV and newspapers show Muslims in a fair way. • Muslims do not belong to Australia. • If I saw a Muslim student being abused in a public place I wouldn't care.	• Most Muslims have good feelings for Australia and Australians. • This school helps people of different cultures to get along better. • Learning about Muslims helps students to understand them better. • A person can be both a good Muslim and a loyal Australian. • Muslims have made a major contribution to Australia. • Most Australians have good feelings for Muslims. • The image of Muslims is as good as other migrant groups in Australia. • Australian schools should teach more about Muslims.

two may work in tandem. This supports a basic notion of the contact hypothesis that suggests that having some contact with others decreases prejudice.

Discussion and Conclusions

The survey found that students are divided in the degree and nature of prejudice and tolerance towards Muslims in Australia.

Boys were less accepting of Muslims and Islam than were girls. Although boys agreed more than girls with the statement, 'Most Muslims treat women with less respect than do other Australians', this was clearly a view not based on direct experience.

There was a strong tendency for the two Christian groups (Catholics and Other Christians) to be significantly less well-disposed towards Muslims and Islam than the Non-religious.

On two statements, all three religious affiliations differed significantly: 'Muslims threaten the Australian way of life', in which all disagreed, but to different degrees (Non-religious most, Catholics next, Other Christians least); all agreed with the statement 'most Muslims treat women with less respect than do other Australians' (Other Christian most, Catholics next, Non-religious least).

Changing patterns of work and communication mean that in the course of their lives young people are likely to meet and interact with people from many

Table 3.3
Difference in Attitude Between Students With or Without Muslim Friends

Those with Muslim friends agreed more, or disagreed less, than those without	Those without Muslim friends agreed more, or disagreed less, than those with
• Muslims have made a major contribution to Australia. • Muslims have made a major contribution to world civilisation. • Most Muslims have good feelings for Australia and Australians. • Most Muslims have stronger family ties than other Australians. • Australian schools should teach more about Muslims. • This school helps people of different cultures to get along better. • Learning about Muslims helps students to understand them better. • A person can be both a good Muslim and a loyal Australian.	• Muslims find it hard to integrate into Australia. • Muslims threaten the Australian way of life. • Most migrants are racist. • Hollywood movies show Muslims in a fair way. • Muslims do not belong to Australia. • If I saw a Muslim student being abused in a public place I wouldn't care

different communities, cultures and backgrounds. What then is the role of schools in promoting intercultural understanding? Is there a role for school-based interfaith programs, intercultural studies, and student welfare programs? Does the school curriculum matter? If not, why not? How can it be made more effective?

Schools have an important role to play in increasing mutual understanding and respect and appreciation of cultural diversity. Eradicating racism and promoting racial equality must be an integral part of school life and should be explicit and implicit in all curriculum activities that take place within the school. National, regional and local initiatives provide support, advice and guidance for schools to ensure all pupils are taught about equality. The National Curriculum guidelines for Citizenship and Personal, Social and Health Education (PSHE) identify what pupils should be taught in association with racial equality and antiracist behaviour.

The degree to which students feel that their school is educative about Muslims and Islam is an important predictor of certain levels of tolerance. This suggests that it is the atmosphere created by the school that is supportive and educative of Muslims and Islam, rather than the level of knowledge that is important regarding prejudice. Therefore, it is not just a matter of knowing more facts about Muslims and Islam but perceiving that the school cares enough to educate students on these issues that is important.

It is worth considering the contribution that outsiders to the education bureaucracy can make, particularly those from the Muslim community, to the development of policies, curriculum materials and pedagogical practices.

Current multicultural policies and students alike appear to de-emphasise knowledge as a means to understanding and cultural harmony, and this appears to be a major problem as we head to the future.

Endnotes

1 These locations were excluded as it would have been costly to survey them for logistical reasons. In any case it was thought they would not contribute to survey accuracy as there was no reason to suppose their responses would differ from those in other states.
2 A pilot study was conducted at nine schools with 552 students, and a short form survey was conducted at 13 schools with 682 students.
3 Table 3.1 was generated with the help of Dean Lusher.

Bibliography

Akbarzadeh, A., & Saeed, S. (Eds.), *Muslim communities in Australia*. Sydney, Australia: UNSW Press.

Asmar, C. (2001). A community on campus: Muslim students in Australian universities. In A. Saeed & S. Akbarzadeh (Eds.), *Muslim communities in Australia* (pp. 138–160). Sydney, Australia: UNSW Press.

Ata, A., & Batrouney, T. (1989). Attitudes and stereotyping in Victorian secondary schools. *The Eastern Anthropologist, 42*(1), 35–50.

Australian Arabic Council. (2001, September). *Increase in racial vilification in light of terror attacks: A media report*. Melbourne, Australia: Author.

Bobo, L., & Hutchings, V. (1996). Perceptions of racial group competition: Extending Blumer's theory of group position to a multiracial social context. *American Sociological Review, 61*, 951–972.

Brasted, H. (2001). Contested representations in historical perspective: Images of Islam and the Australian press 1950–2000. In S. Akbarzadeh & A. Saeed (Eds.), *Muslim communities in Australia*. Sydney, Australia: UNSW Press.

Bullivant, B.M. (1987). *The ethnic encounter in the secondary school: Ethnocultural reproduction and resistance: Theory and case studies*. London; New York: Falmer Press.

Bullivant, B.M. (1988). The ethnic success: Ethical challenges to conventional wisdom about immigrant disadvantages in Australia. *Australian Journal of Education, 32*(2), 223–243.

Cahill, D., & Gundert, A. (1996). *Immigration and schooling in the 1990s*. Canberra, Australia: Australian Government Publishing Service.

Davis, R., & Stimson, R. (1988). Disillusionment and disenchantment at the fringe: Explaining the geography of the one nation party vote at the Queensland election. *People and Place, 6*, 69–82.

Department of Education. (1997). *Multicultural policy for Victorian schools*. Melbourne: Author.

Department of Education. (2003). *Advice for schools in dealing with the international situation*. (School Circular: 075/2003). Melbourne, Australia: Author.

Department of Education and Training. (2000). *Racism. No way: Anti-racism education for Australian schools*. Retrieved January 17, 2006, from http://www.racismnoway.com.au/

Department of Education Employment and Training. (2001). *Guidelines for managing cultural and linguistic diversity in schools*. Melbourne, Australia: Author.

Donohoue Clyne, I. (2000). Seeking education: The struggle of Muslims to educate their children in Australia. PhD thesis, University of Melbourne, Australia.

Donohoue Clyne, I. (2001). Educating Muslim children in Australia. In S. Akbarzadeh & A. Saeed (Eds.), *Muslim communities in Australia*. Sydney, Australia: UNSW Press.

Dunn, K. (2001). The geography of racism in NSW: A theoretical exploration and some preliminary findings from the mid 1990s. *The Australian Geographer, 32*(1), 29–44.

Dunn, K. (2004). Islam in Australia: Contesting the discourse of absence. *The Australian Geographer, 53*(3) pp 333–353.

Dunn, K. (2005). Australian public knowledge of Islam. *Studia Islamika: Indonesian Journal for Islamic Studies, 12*(1), 1–32.

Dunscombe, R. (2004). *Heinemann media 1. Units 1 & 2*. Melbourne, Australia: Heinemann.

Galbally, F. (1978). *Migrant services and programs: Report of the review of post-arrival programs and services for migrants*. Canberra, Australia: Australian Government Printing Service.

Goodall, H., & Jakubowicz, A. (1994). *Racism, ethnicity and the media*. Sydney, Australia: Allen and Unwin.

Human Rights and Equal Opportunity Commission. (2004). *Ismaυ listen: National consultations on eliminating prejudice against Arab and Muslim Australians*. Sydney, Australia: Author.

Kalantzis, M., & Cope, B. (1984). Multiculturalism and education policy. In G. Bottomley & M.M. De Lepervanche (Eds.), *Ethnicity, class and gender in Australia*. Sydney, Australia: George Allen and Unwin.

Muslim Community Reference Group. (2006). *Building on social cohesion, harmony and security*. Canberra, Australia.

Omar, W., Hughes, P.J., & Allen, K. (1996). *The Muslims in Australia*. Canberra, Australia: Australia Government Publishing Service.

Park, R.E., Burgess, E.W., & McKenzie, R.D. (1925). *The city*. Chicago: University of Chicago Press.

Pew Research Centre. (2006). *Conflicting views in a divided world*. Washington, DC: The Pew Global Attitudes Project.

Poynting, S. (2002). Bin Laden in the suburbs: Attacks on Arab and Muslim Australians before and after 11 September. *Current Issues in Criminal Justice, 14*(1), 43–64.

Rieder, J. (1985). *Canarsie: The Jews and Italians of Brooklyn against Liberalism*. Cambridge, MA: Harvard University Press.

Said, E. (1981). *Covering Islam: How the media and the experts determine how we see the rest of the world*. New York: Pantheon Books.

Said, E. (1995). *Orientalism*. New York: Penguin.

Simkin, K., & Gauci, B. (1992). Ethnic diversity and multicultural education. In R.J. Burns & A.R. Welch (Eds.), *Contemporary perspectives in comparative education*. New York: Garland Publications.

Speck, B.W. (1997). Respect for religious differences: The case of Muslim students. *New Directions for Teaching and Learning, 70*, 39–46.

Windle, J. (2004). Schooling, symbolism and social power: The hijab in Republican France. *Australian Educational Researcher, 31*(1), 95–112.

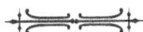

Chapter 4

The Lebanese in Melbourne
Ethnicity, Interethnic Activities and Attitudes to Australia

The main difficulty in presenting a conclusive analysis about the ethnicity of the Lebanese lies in the multiplicity of its definitions. One possible analysis would depend on a 'motivational understanding' of ways that sociologists have chosen to define the context of a particular group under examination, the relationship between a particular group in one instance and other groups in another (Shutz, 1967).[1]

In a definition of ethnicity, Foltz (1974) proposes that through comparison of one's self with the host society, self-consciousness comes into being. However, Foltz does not specify the properties that he had noted earlier, as they vary from one group to another and also from one context to another. For example, because religion is so intertwined with the Lebanese identity, it serves as a meaningful boundary between the Lebanese community and other groups.

The Roots of Lebanese Ethnicity

Historically, the identity of the Lebanese has been primarily based on religious adherence by members of the community to a system of 'millet' during the Ottoman rule between the 14th and 19th centuries. Each of the Christian communities was divided according to both religious and national boundaries. The millets were like states within a state; they had their own taxation system, and their own set of laws. They were like autonomous regions within the Ottoman Empire and were given autonomy in return for unswerving loyalty to the Empire. Hourani (1955, p. 121) summarises the situation in his perception that 'the religious communities were shut off from one another on the levels of belief, personal law, and close personal relations, but on that of economic life they were closely intertwined'.

Table 4.1
Religious Background

Religious background	Frequency	Percentage
Maronite	28	31
Orthodox	21	23
Catholic	13	15
Muslim	21	23
Druze	5	6
Other (Protestant)	2	2
Total	90	100

The predominant and fundamental preoccupation of the Lebanese with sectarian loyalty in the matter of religious faith has been transplanted to their new country. For most Lebanese migrants religious institutions are considered to be centres for cultural, social and psychological pilgrimage. Being identified as Lebanese meant that one's identity is synonymous with affiliation to a particular religion (Sklare, 1957; see Table 4.1). This identification is so strong among the Lebanese that every respondent identified with a particular sect, even though 29% of the sample never attended a Lebanese church (see Table 4.2). However, the groups listed in Table 4.2 display a separate identity, with the exception of 2% who gave a vague response of 'all of the above'. Taking refuge in a non-committal response possibly signifies a negative one: under the pressure of social norms, this group felt under an obligation to indicate some sort of religious affiliation.

Such psychological pressures are explained by Kayal (1975, p. 50), who says that 'the specific differences in religious belief among Jews, Christians and Muslims are not so important as the status and social obligation inherent in being a member of a particular group'. He further states that the West falsely attributes the different social order between the different Lebanese sects to

Table 4.2
Frequency Distribution of Church–Mosque Affiliates (90 Cases)

Religious institutions	%
1. Our Lady of (Maronite) Lebanese	22
2. Saint Joseph (Melkite) Church	10
3. Saint Nicholas (Orthodox) Church	11
4. Saint George's (Orthodox) Church	8
5. The Islamic Mosque	2
6. Roman Catholic and Protestant churches	8
7. None	27
8. All of the above	0
9. Both orthodox churches	2
Total	100

ideological determinants. It is more correct to suppose, as he points out, that 'the theological differences have become translated into social and structural realities with each community becoming socially separate from the others' (Kayal, 1975, p. 50).

The combination of religion and nationality is a form of identification for every Lebanese institution. By law, every Lebanese must be identified by his sect on his passport, as well as on every official document and application form. For some this system has proved an advantage, for others a hindrance.

Such religious and national labelling is still common in the Lebanese community in Melbourne. In my first encounter with a Lebanese priests, he enquired, 'and what is your religion, son?'. He was surprised to find that I was a Protestant and came from Zahle, a town that is traditionally Maronite. The priest then half-jokingly proposed a wedding with 'a nice Maronite girl in order that you might be converted to the Maronite church' (Interview, June 11, 1977).

It is perhaps inevitable that members of different Lebanese sects claim that Lebanon was originally Maronite, Muslim, and so forth. Kayal remarks that 'they speak of their "nation", meaning the church, without realising this is a purely artificial use of the word introduced (originally) by the Muslims and because they had no other way of classifying the Christians' (Kayal, 1975, p. 40).

There remains the question of 'sense of belonging', which is also essentially a byproduct of religion and nationality. If we ask whether the religious background of the Lebanese determines their attitude towards other Lebanese groups, the answer is a definite 'yes'. Hunt and Walker (1974) remark that anyone who claims their identity is Lebanese but originally came from a different minority sect from one's own is viewed as being of 'doubtful loyalty'. It is also rare for a Lebanese person to claim political loyalty differing from that traditionally associated with his religion; for example, an a Lebanese Maronite almost never ascribes to a leftist point of view.

Reasons for Attending Church or Mosque

It is my contention that Lebanese churches and mosques do not reinforce ethnicity through their rituals but are intrinsically social and cultural ethnic institutions. To further understand the acculturation of the Lebanese, the impact of religion on their psychological identity must be taken into account. Gullick (1967, p. 10) has said that, 'religion, religious symbols and sectarian affiliation are so institutionalised in the Lebanese culture that a Lebanese would think twice before crossing them out of his vocabulary'.

When asked the reasons for attending church or mosque, a sizeable proportion of the sample (33%) indicated in various ways that it was because their family or ancestors had done so; these figures support the proposition that for

Table 4.3
Reasons for Attending a Specific Church or Mosque (90 cases)

Reasons	%
Proximity	6
Religious background	33
To meet other Lebanese	3
Feelings of sense of belonging	4
Because of the language	9
Because of Lebanese atmosphere	3
Not applicable	36
In order to pray	3
The priest comes from the same village	2
Total	100

most Lebanese migrants religion is still a matter of ancestry rather than faith (see Table 4.3). It can also be inferred that a large number of Lebanese acquire a functional identity through religious affiliation.

The four Lebanese churches and the mosque have become reassuring institutions for migrants; 3% of respondents attend because the pleasures of social contact take precedence over spiritual matters. Only 3% of those who attend church or mosque stated that 'prayer' was the reason for their attendance. Such a proportion is certainly small in comparison to reasons given for attendance in Western churches. One possible explanation is that, irrespective of inner feelings and belief, the fact remains that the majority of Lebanese feel under strong obligation to identify with their sects publicly (Gullick, 1967). In turn, the Lebanese clergy and religious institutions seem reluctant to tamper with aspects of their services or activities that reinforce Lebanese ethnicity. The reason is that if Lebanese migrants are disappearing as an ethnic community, all of the religious institutions are also likely to disappear; they realise, as I have previously stated, that for the 'average' Lebanese, religion is nationality and provides a vital reference point as far as psychological identity is concerned. Leary (1913, p. 9) remarks that:

> ... every [Lebanese] not only counts himself an adherent of the faith into which he was born, but he thrusts that fact on your attention, and on the slightest provocation, is ready to fight for his belief. A man's ancestors, descendents and home may be cursed with all the wealth of Oriental vituperation, and he will probably accept this as a mere emphatic conversational embellishment. But let the single word 'dinak' — 'the religion' — be spoken with a curseful intonation to a follower of a different faith, and the spirit of murder is let loose.

Two groups comprise those whose response was labelled *Not applicable* (36%): the first consists of 27% who simply do not attend any religious institution; the remaining 9% were unable to state any reason for their attendance. One

Table 4.4
Responses to the Question: 'What Is the Best Thing About Going to Your Church–Mosque?'

Responses	%
Meeting other Lebanese	22
Absence of control by religious leaders	3
It teaches love	3
It makes my parents happy	2
Its leader	6
The service	20
Nothing	4
Don't know	7
Not applicable (do not attend)	32
Total	100

middle-aged man displayed unusual cynicism by stating, 'Two things give you a headache, politics and religion'.

An analysis of the results of Table 4.4 supports an earlier observation that pride in religious identification with co-religionists is a direct outgrowth of the 'millet' system that so rigidly divided religious communities. Table 4.4 shows that as many as 22% indicated that the best thing about attending a church or mosque is 'meeting other Lebanese'. Obviously they consider co-religionists to be 'their people', as if they were members of an extended family. Another 2% gave the response, 'it makes my parents happy'. Interestingly, these respondents were in their mid-30s. Another 6% indicated that the priest or sheikh was the best thing about attending their church or mosque; another 4% attend in order to meet friends. The latter response was given by 22% as a response to the question, 'What is the best thing about attending your church–mosque?' (see Table 4.4). A small proportion (9%) gave language, or rather the inability to speak English, as a reason. It should also be noted that for almost all of those who attend, the various Lebanese religious institutions have become important meeting places wherein to fulfil social obligations.

Village and Kinship Societies

During the past 4 years, there has been a remarkable renaissance of smaller communal societies in the Lebanese communities. Alienated from the Lebanese community at large, migrants who came from the same village began forming their own associations, aimed at pooling financial resources for their relatives in Lebanon. It was also hoped that such coordinated efforts would render effective assistance in sponsoring prospective relative–immigrants. A limited range of activities and absence of meaningful policies, along with irregular and informal meetings, have contributed to a lack of effectiveness in these societies.

Table 4.5
Membership of Australian and Lebanese Clubs

Kinds of clubs	% of membership	
	Australian clubs	Lebanese clubs
1. Sport	12	28
2. Political;	6	13
3. Charitable	1	6
4. Religious	1	3
5. Social	—	1
6. Union	2	—
7. Cultural	—	—
8. None	78	49
Total (n = 90)	100	100

Although a sizeable number of these 'societies' have no official president, any member who enjoys a reasonable degree of authority and status and is older than the rest assumes a de facto position of leadership. Neither education nor linguistic ability are considered relevant. Most of the societies take pride in announcing their formation in various Lebanese newspapers. The Department of Immigration and Ethnic Affairs has a listing of about 50 societies, although some community members estimate the number to exceed 130. It is apparent that these societies reinforce in varying degrees certain religious, political, and ideological sentiments. However, Lebanese migrants in Melbourne are less enthusiastic about joining clubs and societies than they are about being affiliated with their religious institutions, primarily because of the ineffectiveness of various organisations in promoting the welfare of migrants and helping to liaise with government departments.

Table 4.5 shows that approximately one-half of the sample interviewed (49%) are not members of Lebanese clubs or societies. The percentage of political club affiliates (13%) is surprisingly small considering the highly politicised nature of the community. While the ordinary Lebanese is hypersensitive about revealing his political views, religio–political sentiments seem to shape his general lifestyle.

Relationship With Australians

Results in Table 4.5 reveal that those who are not members of Australian clubs (78%) far outnumber 'non-participants' in Lebanese clubs (49%). While the majority of Lebanese have absolutely no contact with such Australian institutions, it is assumed that the remainder (22%) successfully interact to some extent with Australians — whether in political parties (6%), sporting clubs (12%), charitable organisations (1%), religious institutions (1%) or unions (2%). Interestingly, of the 22% who are members of Australian social organ-

Table 4.6
Lebanese Households Visited by Sample on a Monthly Basis

Percentage of other Lebanese households of total number of visiting 'mixed' families visited per month	Respondents
10	4
20	2
30	2
40	1
50	7
60	2
70	3
80	6
90	17
100 (all)	43
None at all	3

Note: n = 90 cases

isations, one happens to be the president of a local bowls club, and another is the secretary of a golf club. The former migrated to Australia in 1953 and enjoys an upper-middle-class lifestyle in the affluent Melbourne suburb of Kew. In a moment of introspection he remarked: 'I spoke English fluently before migrating to Australia; but only when I transcended the social class barrier was I encouraged to feel part of other Australians' lives that in turn made us have minimal contact with other Lebanese' (interview 57).

As over 50% of the Lebanese are both non-members of Australian and Lebanese organisations, the term 'marginal' may be applicable to them. Although most Lebanese enjoy communication with friends or relatives, a few must obviously feel alienated in their unfamiliar surroundings. Yet, so long as they can consider themselves 'sojourners', that is, temporary residents, this can be withstood (64% of the sample indicated uncertainty about permanent settlement in Australia).

Results shown in Table 4.6 tend to support the assumption that despite the residentially scattered nature of the community, social interaction among the Lebanese is common. As many as 8.5% of the sample interact with more Lebanese families than they do Australian families or families from other ethnic groups. As over 50% of the number of families visited every month by 8.5% of the sample are Lebanese, it is fair to assume these figures reflect feelings of togetherness among kinship members rather than social cohesion of the Lebanese community as a whole. More importantly, a sizeable total of 43 respondents (approximately 46%) indicated that all of the families they visited are Lebanese.

A similar study by Jones (1962) shows that kinship ties were one of the major factors that dominated the visitation features among Italians in the suburb of Carlton in Melbourne. He states that it not only provided them with a sense of togetherness, but also reinforced their intermarriage relationships. With respect to social activities, as with Sweet's (1974) findings on the Lebanese in Edmonton, the Lebanese in Melbourne are observed during social functions to practise the traditional etiquette and emotional speeches they would use at a similar occasion in Lebanon. Each of the local Lebanese societies tend to have a hierarchical social structure, reflecting that of the Lebanese village society. If decisions are to be made, advice is sought first from an elderly male. Kinship ties are so strong that intermarriage rarely extends beyond the boundaries of the extended family. It was found that out of the 58 married couples interviewed, as many as 39 (67%) wives and husbands were born in the same village.

Superficially, it may appear that the local Lebanese community that was not accustomed to paying taxes in Lebanon is now acculturated, in that it has adjusted to Australian conditions such as paying taxes, voting, and becoming naturalised. Nevertheless, traditional values and habits continue to characterise their everyday behaviour. As only a minority has successfully integrated into the lifestyle of Australian society, the theme of continuity that was illustrated at the outset of the present work must be emphasised here. More importantly, maintenance of kinship structure and solidarity among its members, ineffective as it may be in creating a feeling of larger 'Lebanese' identity rather than sectarian identity, and despite the pressures placed on it in a Western urbanised society, still proves an effective barrier to assimilation, for the present time at least.

Attitudes to Australia

Apart from the responses to questions (6) the weather, and (9) the degree of political freedom in Table 4.7, the migrants sampled found things worse or better than they had expected in roughly equal numbers.

Furthermore, the figures suggest that there is a high proportion of Lebanese who had absolutely no idea about Australia or were too young to have formed any expectations before migration. While a large number had no expectations concerning discrimination (66%), ease of making friends (58%), and degree of political freedom (58%), some 64% had given some thought to gaining employment. Those who had not considered the question were too young to do so at the time of migration. The highest proportion of responses (19%) implying disappointment was related to not finding employment easily. Concerning 'the degree of political freedom', as many as 18% found it better than they had expected, while only 3% found it worse. Obviously the rigidity and instability of the 'perfect' political system in Lebanon is a major factor

Table 4.7
Attitudes to Australia: Disparity Between Expectations (Premigration) and Realisations (Postmigration — 90 Case)

Q: 'You must have had some idea about the things listed below before migration. How did you find them after arrival?'

	Better than I expected %	The same %	Worse than I expected %	Don't know I was too young %
Standard of living	22	26	18	34
Standard of accommodation	16	23	17	44
Case of finding employment	23	32	19	26
Interest in job	14	27	16	43
Quality of medical care	13	20	8	59
The weather	2	42	19	37
Sense of belonging	10	23	9	58
Ease of making friends	13	13	16	58
Degree of political freedom	18	21	3	58
Amount of leisure	12	24	13	49
Discrimination	10	14	10	66

behind such responses. On arrival, the Lebanese migrant is stunned by the fact that he is no longer pressured to vote in a particular way.

Favourable Aspects of the Australian Culture

The limited number of items in Table 4.7 prompted the introduction of an open-ended question. The variety of responses obtained to the question, 'What do you think is the best thing about living in Australia?' is outlined in Table 4.8.

These responses are the outcome of statements that range from the very accurate and articulate to the vague and confused. For example, the following response was obtained in reply to the original question:

> As you and I know ... in Australia you can do anything you like as long as you don't make a mistake. Nobody tells you what to do ... where you are going or coming ... why you don't like the Prime Minister. Over there (in Lebanon) if the police dislike you they will put you in jail.

The concept of social services is quite alien to the Lebanese. The system in Lebanon is based on a capitalistic form of free enterprise that dispenses with collection of income taxes. The economically deprived (who could be said to make up approximately 90% of the population) suffer the burden of astronomical hospital, medical, and educational fees. The relatively high response rate regarding social justice (11 persons) and security of living (13 persons) is thus quite understandable.

Table 4.8
Favourable Aspects of the Australian Culture

Responses	Frequency
Freedom	23
Social justice, law and order	11
Security of living	13
Employment opportunities	6
Peace	8
Individual rights and privacy	5
Standard of living	3
Social services	5
Friendliness and informality	3
Opportunities in education	1
Straightforwardness	2
Generosity to the needy	1
Making money	1
Absence of religious discrimination	1
Cleanliness	1
Absolutely nothing	3
Everything	1
Do not know	1
Absence of racial discrimination	1

Unfavourable Aspects of the Australian Culture

As with favourable responses, the replies concerning the unfavourable aspects of Australian culture, as shown in Table 4.9, were numerous and diverse. It was necessary to aggregate such responses into further categories for the purpose of cross-tabulation. The responses are examined in detail in Table 4.10, taking into account crucial factors such as educational background and age differences. The results suggest that the responses vary according to the level of education received.

It should be noted that despite the apparent variation in the responses, they were initially aggregated for the purpose of an effective cross-tabulation. The original responses were given in a more elaborate form than in the following examples:

> Friendship with Australians is easy to make, easy to lose.
>
> We have tried the lot ... we invite them to our house, they never show up ... and if we talk to them they open the door a little but they never let you in ... still, it is their country.

These comments are typical of the culture shock that most migrants experience when values of the host culture are perceived to contradict those of their traditional social upbringing. In Lebanon, because informal modes of communication cut across civil, official, legal, departmental and institutional spheres, one's private affairs are considered to be of public interest. More often than not

Table 4.9
Unfavourable Aspects of the Australian Culture

Frequency of responses	Response
Lack of family ties; lax familial discipline	7
Hedonism, materialism	1
Sexual permissiveness	17
Necessity to compromise Lebanese identity	4
Inflation	5
Excessive emphasis on sport	1
Discrimination	8
Neglect of the aged	1
Drunkenness	4
Divorce rate	1
Trivial lifestyle	5
Weather	5
Apathy towards migrants	2
Do not know	2
Nothing	4
Fragmentation of social ties	13
Taxes	2
Lack of free time	3
Poor medical care	1
Delinquency	1
Impoliteness	1
Factory work	1
Everything	1

Table 4.10
Unfavourable Aspects of the Australian Culture and Level of Education

| Unfavourable aspects | Level of formal education in % | | | |
	None	Primary	Secondary	Tertiary
No opinion, or nothing	25	57	5	—
Sexual permissiveness	37.5	23.3	17	—
Unfriendliness	—	20	32.5	75
Lack of spiritual values	25	33.3	22.5	16.7
Other responses	12.5	16.7	22.5	8.3

when a person applies for a job, he is expected to reveal his relationship with his friends, neighbours and relatives, what assets he owns, his political affiliations and other information that in Australia would be considered irrelevant if not unlawful. It is therefore understandable why a Lebanese migrant is baffled by the transitory nature of his relationships with Australians whom he encounters socially or at work.

The typical generosity of Lebanese in social relationships has been a major factor in contributing to stunned reactions towards Australians' more inhibited attitudes. One Lebanese worker remarked, 'In the pub, I never let an Australian "friend" pay for his drinks ... but if he offers me a glass he always says, "Your shout next, mate"'.

Lack of Spiritual Values

A common response in this category related to what the Lebanese consider a lack of family ties and lax upbringing of children (Table 4.9). Of the seven respondents who gave this reply the following remarks may be considered typical:

> When their [Australian] children begin to earn money they don't know their parents any more. So they take drugs, drink and 'bludge' around ... or they form gangs and tease everyone in the street ... Don't worry, my girl is doing the same now. She always wants to do things privately and by herself.

With respect to responses registered regarding 'hedonism' or 'materialism' as the worst aspect of the Australian culture, there is a major gulf.

The proportion of respondents who had received tertiary education regarded 'unfriendliness' as the most unfavourable aspect of Australian culture (75%); this percentage was much lower among secondary-educated (32.5%) and primary-educated respondents. Those with a higher level of education are more sensitive towards matters involving social relationships. Other responses, such as 'lack of spiritual values' (16.7%) and 'other' (8.3%), were less significant to these respondents. Of the respondents who had received no formal education unfriendliness was not considered to be an unfavourable aspect of Australian culture, possibly because more immediate needs made this less significant.

Concerning 'sexual permissiveness' the reverse pattern is observed. While those with no formal education rated such matters as most important (37%), this percentage decreased as formal education increased; no tertiary-educated respondents considered this to be an unfavourable aspect of Australian culture. With the exception of 'other responses', similar patterns of response are observed in relation to the other categories.

According to the t test (0.4), there is a significant relationship between responses to unfavourable aspects of the Australian culture and the age of the respondents.

The results in Table 4.11 reveal that while 30.4% of older people (31–68 years) considered 'lack of spiritual values' to be the outstanding unfavourable aspect of Australia, younger persons (40.9%) confined most of their responses to what they saw as 'unfriendliness'.

Younger Lebanese seem to hold strong opinions on Australia, as indicated by their zero response in the *No opinion* category, in contrast to 13% by the older age group.

Sexual Permissiveness

The high proportion of responses (17) given to 'sexual permissiveness' as the worst aspect of the Australian culture (Table 4.9), would seem to warrant some

Table 4.11
Unfavourable Aspects of the Australian Culture by Age

Unfavourable aspects	18–30 years 'young' in %	31–68 years 'old' in %
Sexual permissiveness	15.9	21.6
Unfriendliness	40.9	71.7
Lack of spiritual values	20.5	30.4
Other responses	22.7	13.1
Don't know — nothing	—	13.1

Note: χ^2 = 17.55093, df = 9, Cramers V = .26391, Significance = .04, n = 90.

investigation. The polarised sexual attitudes between a sexually restrictive Lebanese society and a permissive Australian society are probably the major factor behind such responses. In most Middle Eastern cultures, the rigid code of male honour (ird) has determined both the destiny and behaviour of women. As an example of the gulf between the sexual mores of the two cultures, one may take the seemingly trivial example of the wearing of trousers by females. In the Middle East, the wearing of such attire is condemned by conservative villagers, both because of its sexual 'suggestiveness' and because of its implications of challenge to male supremacy. One can imagine the reaction of an average Lebanese male towards the fact that his daughter wears trousers. For him it is inconceivable that a decent girl should dress in such a way as to make herself sexually attractive. 'Why should she exhibit her charms if she does not mean to sell or give them away?' is a question that is unanswerable, given the thought processes of a conservative male Arab.

In the absence of sexual instruction in schools, Lebanese children are faced with an overpowering dilemma that their Australian counterparts rarely experience. Normal adolescent sexual awareness causes guilt feelings as a result of the restrictive mores that girls especially are taught at home, which is so much at odds with the outlook of their Australian peers; the mental and psychological confusion that results is understandable. Because the school environment is often regarded as a threat to chastity, two Lebanese families who came to my notice withdrew their daughters from school at the age of 13 (Conway (1971).[2] One of the parents rationalised his action in the following terms: 'We need her more at the shop ... She might marry next year and we will never see her again' (Interview 11).

Complaints that the Australian emphasis on sexual equality would eventually defeminise women were often heard. Complaints concerning 'sexual permissiveness' on the part of males must be considered against the background of complete subordination of females in Middle Eastern societies; a society such as Australia's, which tolerates sexual freedom for women, offers many bewildering challenges to the Lebanese male, whether he is single, a husband, or the father of a daughter. Lebanese women have been unable to compete on an economic or social level with men or display any 'masculine' qualities.

Community leaders, both religious and academic, reinforce the notions that men and women are by nature unequal with respect to their physical strength and also in their mental capacity and temperament.

Of course, a sexual double standard flourishes in the Lebanese community, as noted by a Lebanese–Australian doctor:

> Our men convey an impression of decency and religiosity by sheltering their wives at home ... In the most secret circumstances, they continue to seek treatment for venereal diseases that they have obtained from 'places of entertainment' ... their wives become infected as a result, and the repercussions are obvious — severe infection or divorce. (Interview, May 6, 1977.)

Unfriendliness, informality

This category of responses includes fragmentation of social ties (13), impoliteness (1), apathy towards migrants (2), discrimination (8), and necessity to compromise Lebanese identity (4). Despite the apparent variation in substance of the responses, they are initially aggregated for the purpose of an effective cross-tabulation. Lack of family ties and fragmentation of social ones rank highest.

With respect to responses registered regarding 'hedonism' or 'materialism' as the worse aspect of the Australian culture there is a gulf between Lebanese and Australian attitudes regarding the purpose of material possessions. Conway (1971, p. 91) contends the typical Australian father who directs his efforts to buying such possessions as a car or a house is not left 'with a wide scope for any domestic interest; since his role is primarily that of the provider'. Thus, while 'the materialistic traditions of the Australian community impose a convention of 'ideal' family life based on getting concrete possessions' (Conway, 1971, p. 91) is a fine observation, the primary concern of the Lebanese breadwinner is, first and foremost, to maintain a traditional structure among members of the extended family.

Other Responses

This category consists of responses that are largely unrelated and too distinct to warrant inclusion in the three previous categories. Some of the responses are: 'inflation', 'taxes', 'weather', 'medication', 'nothing', 'everything', 'I don't know'. In the latter group, the following response was recorded: 'This is my eighth year in the factory — and it's good ... What will I do back in Lebanon, everyone is fighting ... everything is good here' (Interview 34).

Attitudes to Discrimination

In order to examine how the Lebanese community perceives the reactions of Australians towards migrant groups, the following question was asked: 'What do you think is the general attitude of most Australians towards migrants?' (Table 4.12). As this research did not aim to examine the degree of assimilation of the Lebanese community (a minority group of relatively small size and short history), it is hoped the responses listed below will prove of some assistance in the framework of future research into the question.

Adverse Reactions

Under this category as many as 26 respondents (Table 4.12) indicated that most Australians are either 'resentful' or 'jealous' towards migrants because of fear of competition in the workforce. One respondent remarked that Australians 'see that we work hard for 3 or 4 years and then buy our own house ... Of course they are jealous in that they don't want to work hard and they don't care about their family or anything' (Interview 46). And another: 'We have a good reputation in every country except here ... they don't know that in Beirut skyscrapers are taller than [these in] Melbourne' (Interview 60).

Other Negative Reactions

This category incorporated negative responses with regard to Australian attitudes towards migrants as perceived by the sample. These responses are illustrated in Table 4.12 and range from 'superiority' in attitudes to complete lack of acceptance. It seems, however, that in a number of instances some Lebanese have been either hypersensitive or mistaken about what they perceive as discrimination. One middle-aged Lebanese who sought treatment for his headache complained at hospital:

> She [the nurse] waved for me to sit on a chair. I sat there for 3 hours but she never came back ... I walked to the man with a white coat, but he said he was the cleaner. I did not believe him ... I screamed in Arabic until a few nurses arrived ... I didn't care ... I went outside. In Lebanon if your finger is bleeding, the doctor treats you before anyone else.

Differences in modes of behaviour, communication and codes of ethics have further aggravated unfavourable reactions and feelings of unease. For example, although Australians are content with verbal greetings in casual encounters, to a Lebanese anything less than a handshake is considered unfriendly.

Qualified Negative Reactions

Under this category falls the majority of Lebanese interviewed who tended to qualify their responses. 'Educated Australians look favourably on migrants but not uneducated ones' (Table 4.12) could be considered a typical response in

Table 4.12
Response to the Question: 'What Do You Think is the General Attitude of Australians Towards Migrants?'

Aggregate responses	Actual responses	Frequency of responses
Favourable attitudes	1. Very good, full acceptance	2
	2. Fair to moderate	6
Adverse reactions	3. Resentment–competition in jobs	20
	4. Jealousy	6
'Other' negative reactions	5. Superior attitudes: treating migrants as refugees	10
	6. Avoidance	3
	7. Apathy and insensitivity	5
	8. Rejection: non-acceptance	5
'Qualified' negative reactions	9. OK in the past — not now	1
	10. Young Australians OK — not old ones	1
	11. Minority of Australians good — not majority	8
	12. Uneducated bad — educated good	5
	13. A majority of Australians dislike a minority of migrants	5
	14. Government officials OK — not the public	4
	15. Upper classes OK — not lower	2
	16. Other migrants OK not Australians	1
Not applicable	17. Do not know	6

this category. The fact that a sizeable number of Lebanese are able to discriminate between different classes of Australian society may be considered a favourable development.

Favourable Attitudes

In spite of the overall diversity of responses a very small number (8 respondents) indicated that attitudes of Australians towards migrants were favourable. While this group is comparatively small in size, its members most certainly feel that they themselves are fully accepted by Australians and reflect a tendency to become more assimilated than other groups.

Summary and Conclusions

Throughout this study the term 'Lebanese ethnic community' was used as a term to signify members of a specific community who identify themselves in sectarian terms that makes them distinct from other ethnic minorities.

To a large extent, the functional and structural networks of kinship, the emergence of a number of village societies and strong maintenance of links with the homeland, particularly through the local newspapers, may be symptomatic of alienation to the prospect of permanent settlement. It is observed that as many as 42% indicated that their settlement in Australia was temporary.

The enormous differences between aspects of the Australian and Lebanese culture have been cited as a major factor in creating negative reactions toward Australia in the Lebanese community.

It should be emphasised that while a sizeable proportion of the sample perceived the general attitudes of Australians to migrants (Lebanese inclusive) were negative overall, many qualified their responses in that they felt only a certain segment of the society displays negative reactions to them.

Expectations prior to migration cannot provide us with a sound theoretical framework from which distinctions between the attitudes of Lebanese and those of other migrant groups could be drawn unless it is contrived from broad and generalised theories of assimilation.

Endnotes

1 The findings in tables in this chapter are based on a research survey of 100 Lebanese households. The survey was conducted in the Melbourne metropolitan area in the early 1980s.

2 The author observes that migrant children mature physically at least 2 years earlier than Australian children. This fact prompted concern over the sudden maturity of females.

References

Conway, R. (1971). *The great Australian stupor*. Melbourne, Australia: SunBooks.

Foltz, W.J. (1974). Ethnicity, status and conflict. In W. Bell & W. Freeman (Eds.), *Ethnicity and nation building* (p. 103). Beverly Hills, CA: Sage Publications.

Gullick, J. (1967). *Tripoli, a Moslem Arab city*. Cambridge, MA: Harvard.

Hourani, A. (1955). Race and related ideas in the Near East. In A. Lind (Ed.), *Race relations in world perceptions* (pp. 116–144). Honolulu: University of Hawaii Press.

Hunt, C., & Walker, L (1974). *Ethnic dynamics: Patterns of intergroup relations in various societies*. Homewood, IL: The Dorsey Press.

Jones, F.L. (1962). *Italian population in Carlton: A demographic and sociological survey*. Unpublished doctoral dissertation Canberra, Australian National University, Australia.

Kayal, P. (1975). *The Syrian Lebanese in America*. Boston, MA: Twayne.

Leary, L. (1913). *Syria: The land of Lebanon*. New York: McBride Publication.

Shutz, A. (1967). The phenomenology of the social world. Ivanstown: Cambridge University Press.

Sklare, M. (1957). The function of ethnic churches. In J. Yinger (Ed.), *Religion, society and the individual* (pp. 459–460). New York: MacMillan.

Sweet, L. (1974). Reconstituting a Lebanese society in a Canadian city. In B. Aswad (Ed.), *Arabic speaking communities in American cities* (p. 41). New York: Center for Migration Studies.

Section Two

Education

Chapter 5

The Role of Gender, Religion and Friendship in the Perception of the 'Other'
An Investigation of Secondary Students in Australia: A National Survey

Social scientists agree that a preconceived judgment of how the individual thinks about 'the other' is usually formed without adequate information. This signifies that one draws on his/her prior knowledge as a result of an urgent need to categorise, judge or form an opinion of 'other' individuals; subsequently pronouncing everyone as prejudiced in one form or another (Hutnik, 1991; Hunt et al., 2006; Berzonsky, 2004).

Cultural values and beliefs usually reinforce the interests of the dominant group at the expense of the subdominant; the 'us' and 'them' mentality, where one's own religious or racial group is self-ranked at a higher, better, finer, or more advanced level of lifestyle, morality and thought.

One of these involves measurement of manifest stereotypic behaviour, otherwise defined as the tendency to over-generalise qualities of others. When driven by prejudice, over-generalised qualities are often combined with hostility. The other two approaches measure how an individual relates to a perceived 'other', and the way an individual feels about the 'other'.

Although anti-discrimination laws have been introduced in recent times against organisational practices and procedures used to either directly or indirectly discriminate against 'others', 'polite' prejudice or racism is characteristically rife. Attempts to disguise a dislike of others through a non-prejudicial appearance, or derogatory comments made in private, no longer cause a strain.

Building on Allport's (1954) analysis of prejudice, theorists such as Pettigrew and Meertens (1997) make a theoretical, but not empirically deduced, distinction between subtle and blatant prejudice. The two are 'related but separate' multi-dimensional constructs. By using scores on blatant and subtle measures of their respondents, they found that there were differences between the bigots (scoring high on both measures); subtles (high on subtle, low on blatant); and equalitarians (low on both). The bigots largely attributed negative descriptors to the 'other'; whereas the subtles omitted positive attributes. (Augoustinos and Reynolds, 2001).

Alongside such stereotypes, members of the mainstream (dominant) social group share 'symbolic beliefs' that they value and defend against outgroups (Esses, Haddock, & Zanna, 1993, p. 139; Schwartz & Struch, 1989). These symbolic beliefs consist of a wide variety of perceptions, including the way certain groups fit into their society and help to make it a better or worse place in which to live. According to Esses et al., it is the dissimilarity of such beliefs, rather than ethnocultural characteristics, that induces prejudices and negative attitudes toward other groups. Such assumed differences of the hierarchy of these beliefs raise suspicions and thus lead to intergroup conflicts. In these conflicts, group members perceive not only themselves but also their values to be under threat. And when the group's shared values or symbolic beliefs are (or seem to be) threatened, they tend to become even more salient.

Social walls may be erected both by the minority group to stop its members from assimilating, or by the majority group to prevent minorities from joining them (Hutnik, 1991). Both expressions of prejudice to the 'other' are usually supported by the norms of the community — a church, mosque or temple, a school, workplace, or other institutions. The intensity of it varies with the degree that people want to feel accepted by those around them, and their resistance to the social walls becoming penetrable.

Psychological factors, although very important, constitute only one aspect of the 'us-and-them' conflict. They are interlinked with other factors: political, economic, historical, and so on. Psychological theories are therefore not adequate to explain the intergroup conflict on their own; they reinforce those factors and they are reinforced by them.

The aim of the survey described in this chapter is to probe the attitudes of senior students in Australian schools to Islam and Muslims. It will investigate the extent of Islam-phobia among Australian adolescents and the variation within the gender, religious and friendship divide in the perception of the Muslim community and other selected religious groups.

The findings will provide empirical data to enable a distinction between subtle and blatant prejudice, further contributing to the understanding of the psychosocial development of prejudice.

Without constructing a theoretical model on the basis of statistical findings it is difficult to interpret the problems under examination in this investigation. The temptation to advance theoretical premises without regard to the circumstances surrounding the study would tend to influence the analysis of the statistical results, as well as the interpretation of the attitudinal trends and patterns between the subgroups.

Method

Participants were students from 42 high schools across Australia, with the exception of, for reasons of distance and cost, Western Australia and the Northern Territory. About half the sample came from Catholic schools (53%), and roughly one-quarter each from other Christian schools (26%) and non-denominational schools (21%); only three government schools participated. A total of 2,300 secondary students from Years 10 to 12 completed the questionnaire for this study. Neither Islamic nor Jewish schools were approached to take part in the study.

The survey consisted of a structured questionnaire containing 70 items, including attitudinal, behavioural, knowledge, and demographic details. In addition, participants were presented with attitudinal statements answered by way of a 5-point Likert scale, ranging from 1 (*strongly agree*) to 5 (*strongly disagree*); knowledge of Islam will not be dealt with in this chapter.

Results

The aim of the survey was to explore the attitudes of the sample. Participants were also presented with a list of 15 attributes and asked whether or not each applied respectively to Muslims, Christians and non-religious persons. (The latter two groups were included in order to serve as a baseline against which to compare perceptions of Muslims.)

But does this mask differences within the sample? For instance, do boys differ systematically from girls in their attitudes towards Islam and Muslims? To answer this and similar questions, statistical techniques were used to determine if there were significant differences in the mean attitudes of all the demographic groups measured in the survey.

Gender differences

Significant differences were found between the responses of boys and girls (Figure 5.1). Boys and girls differed significantly statements shown in Table 5.1.

These findings show that boys were less accepting of Muslims and Islam than were girls. Also, as observed in Chapter 3, boys agreed more than girls with the statement, 'Most Muslims treat women with less respect than do other Australians' — clearly a view not based on direct experience.

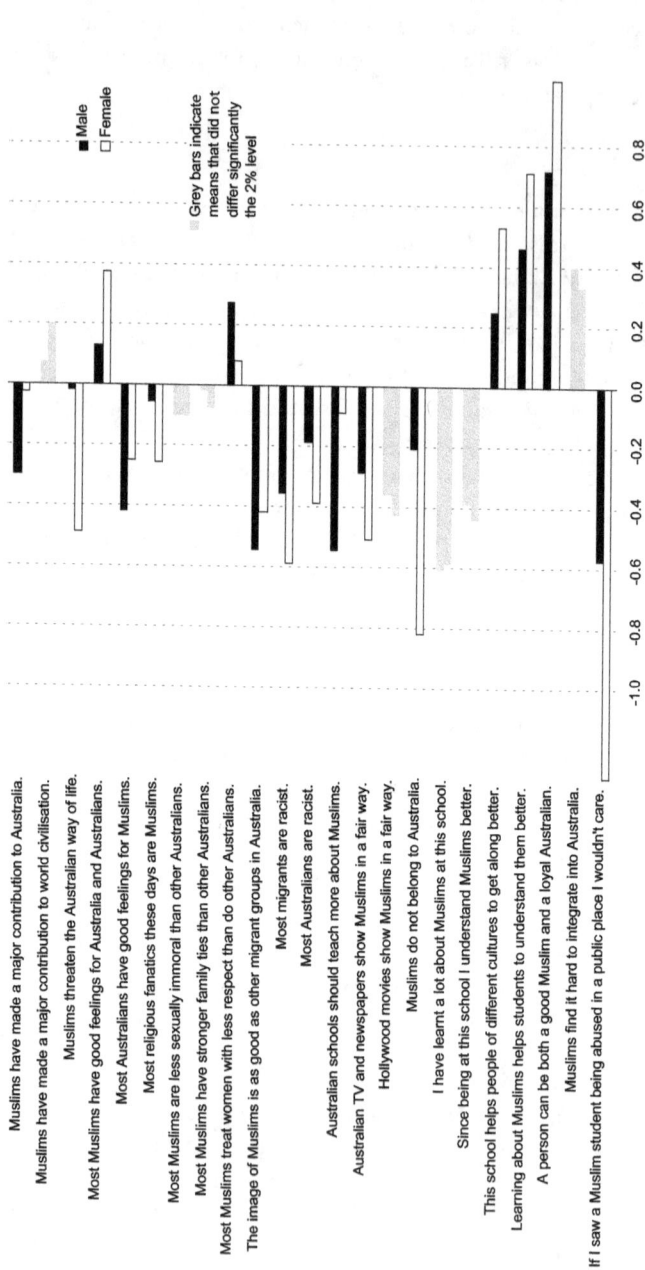

Figure 5.1
Gender differences

Table 5.1
Gender Differences

Boys agreed more, or disagreed less, than girls	Girls agreed more, or disagreed less, than boys
• Most Muslims treat women with less respect than do other Australians. • Muslims threaten the Australian way of life. • Most religious fanatics these days are Muslims. • Most migrants are racist. • Most Australians are racist. • Australian TV and newspapers show Muslims in a fair way. • Muslims do not belong to Australia. • If I saw a Muslim student being abused in a public place I wouldn't care.	• Most Muslims have good feelings for Australia and Australians. • This school helps people of different cultures to get along better. • Learning about Muslims helps students to understand them better. • A person can be both a good Muslim and a loyal Australian. • Muslims have made a major contribution to Australia. • Most Australians have good feelings for Muslims. • The image of Muslims is as good as other migrant groups in Australia. • Australian schools should teach more about Muslims.

The role of religion

Significant differences were found between the responses of respondents according to their religious affiliation (or lack of one; see Figure 5.2).

On many statements, there was a strong tendency for the two Christian groups — Catholics and Other Christians — to resemble each other and to differ from the non-religious group as indicated in Table 5.2.

On two statements, all three religious affiliations differed significantly from each other. Regarding the statement, 'Muslims threaten the Australian way of life', all disagreed, but to different degrees: Non-religious most, Catholics next, Other Christians least. Regarding the statement, 'Most Muslims treat women

Table 5.2
The Role of Religion

Non-religious agreed more, or disagreed less, than Christians	Christians agreed more, or disagreed less, than Non-religious
• Muslims have made a major contribution to world civilisation. • Muslims have made a major contribution to Australia. • Most Muslims have good feelings for Australia and Australians. • Australian schools should teach more about Muslims.	• Most religious fanatics these days are Muslims. • Most migrants are racist. • Muslims do not belong to Australia.

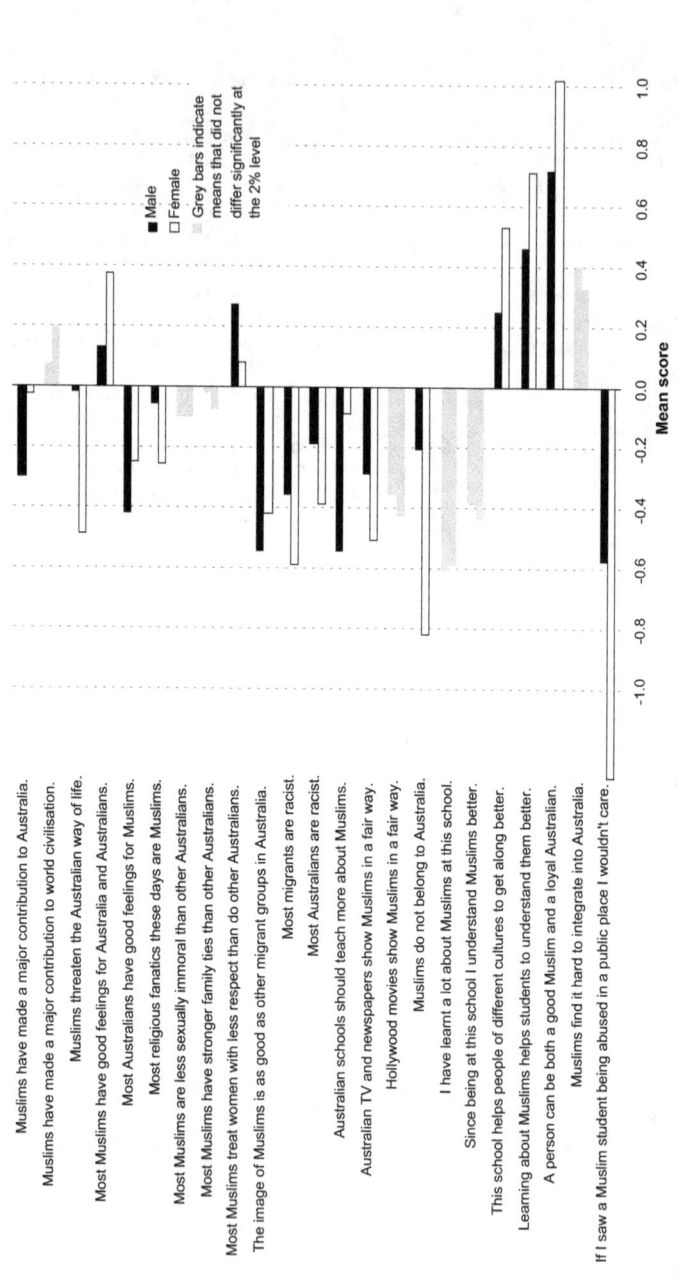

Figure 5.2
Mean attitude scores, by religion

Table 5.3
Differences Between Those With or Without Muslim Friends

Those with Muslim friends agreed more, or disagreed less, than those without	Those without Muslim friends agreed more, or disagreed less, than those with
• Muslims have made a major contribution to Australia. • Muslims have made a major contribution to world civilisation. • Most Muslims have good feelings for Australia and Australians. • Most Muslims have stronger family ties than other Australians. • Australian schools should teach more about Muslims. • This school helps people of different cultures to get along better. • Learning about Muslims helps students to understand them better. • A person can be both a good Muslim and a loyal Australian.	• Muslims find it hard to integrate into Australia. • Muslims threaten the Australian way of life. • Most migrants are racist. • Hollywood movies show Muslims in a fair way. • Muslims do not belong to Australia. • If I saw a Muslim student being abused in a public place I wouldn't care

with less respect than do other Australians', they all agreed: Other Christian most, Catholics next, Non-religious least.

On one statement, 'Australian TV and newspapers show Muslims in a fair way', Other Christian and Non-religious did not differ significantly, but did differ from Catholics: all groups disagreed, Catholics least.

These findings show that the two Christian groups were significantly less well disposed towards Muslims and Islam than were the Non-religious.

Does having Muslim friends make a difference?

In a word, yes. Significant differences were found between the responses of those with Muslim friends and those without (Table 5.3). Those with Muslim friends differed significantly from those without on the statements listed in Table 5.4.

These findings suggest that those with Muslim friends tend to endorse positive attitudes towards Muslims; and although those who lack Muslim friends do not mostly endorse negative attitudes, they do tend to disagree less with them. In other words, positive attitudes are generally embraced by both groups, but more strongly by those with Muslim friends; and negative attitudes are generally opposed by both groups, but more strongly by those with Muslim friends.

Note that these findings say nothing about causation. Having Muslim friends might give rise to positive attitudes, or, alternatively, having positive attitudes might predispose one to seek or accept Muslim friends. Nevertheless,

Table 5.4
Mean Scores Difference in Gender and Religion to Select Attitudes

	Sex			Religion				Father's place of birth			Do you have any Muslim friends?		
	Male	Female	Sig.	Catholic	Other Christian	Not religious	Sig.	Australia	Other	Sig.	Yes	No	Sig.
Attitudes towards Islam and Muslims													
Muslims have made a major contribution to Australia.	2.70	2.97	0.00	2.81	2.82	3.05	0.00	2.82	3.03	0.00	3.31	2.75	0.00
Muslims have made a major contribution to world civilisation.	3.07	3.20	0.04	3.12	3.04	3.37	0.00	3.12	3.28	0.02	3.47	3.06	0.00
Muslims threaten the Australian way of life.	2.94	2.40	0.00	2.63	2.79	2.23	0.00	2.62	2.44	0.02	2.19	2.69	0.00
Most Muslims have good feelings for Australia and Australians.	3.13	3.37	0.00	3.31	3.17	3.41	0.02	3.31	3.26	0.43	3.53	3.22	0.00
Most Australians have good feelings for Muslims.	2.64	2.78	0.02	2.70	2.76	2.74	0.67	2.76	2.64	0.07	2.84	2.69	0.04
Most religious fanatics these days are Muslims.	2.95	2.69	0.00	2.84	2.87	2.57	0.00	2.79	2.76	0.67	2.65	2.82	0.02
Most Muslims are less sexually immoral than other Australians.	2.89	2.92	0.60	2.86	2.93	2.96	0.30	2.90	2.94	0.58	2.86	2.92	0.33
Most Muslims have stronger family ties than other Australians.	2.97	3.03	0.40	2.99	3.02	3.05	0.76	2.99	3.06	0.38	3.10	2.98	0.12
Most Muslims treat women with less respect …	3.29	3.11	0.01	3.21	3.28	3.00	0.01	3.20	3.08	0.09	3.05	3.21	0.05
The image of Muslims is as good as other migrant groups …	2.37	2.60	0.00	2.53	2.51	2.50	0.93	2.52	2.51	0.89	2.52	2.52	0.94
Most migrants are racist.	2.64	2.41	0.00	2.54	2.58	2.29	0.00	2.52	2.40	0.08	2.32	2.54	0.00
Most Australians are racist.	2.81	2.61	0.01	2.69	2.71	2.62	0.58	2.63	2.81	0.02	2.78	2.65	0.12
Australian schools should teach more about Muslims.	2.45	2.91	0.00	2.69	2.65	2.97	0.00	2.73	2.84	0.18	3.19	2.62	0.00
Australian TV and newspapers show Muslims in a fair way.	2.71	2.49	0.00	2.67	2.51	2.40	0.00	2.62	2.40	0.00	2.44	2.60	0.02
Hollywood movies show Muslims in a fair way.	2.64	2.57	0.22	2.63	2.60	2.49	0.14	2.63	2.47	0.01	2.38	2.65	0.00
Muslims do not belong to Australia.	2.79	2.18	0.00	2.51	2.40	2.10	0.00	2.48	2.12	0.00	1.85	2.54	0.00

Table 5.4 continued
Mean Scores Difference in Gender and Religion to Select Attitudes

	Sex			Religion				Father's place of birth			Do you have any Muslim friends?		
	Male	Female	Sig.	Catholic	Other Christian	Not religious	Sig.	Australia	Other	Sig.	Yes	No	Sig.
I have learnt a lot about Muslims at this school.	2.39	2.41	0.87	2.46	2.32	2.39	0.21	2.39	2.44	0.49	2.50	2.37	0.09
Since being at this school I understand Muslims better.	2.61	2.56	0.52	2.66	2.50	2.53	0.10	2.57	2.60	0.79	2.69	2.54	0.07
This school helps people of different cultures to get along better.	3.25	3.53	0.00	3.40	3.48	3.45	0.57	3.40	3.55	0.04	3.64	3.38	0.00
Learning about Muslims helps students to understand ….	3.46	3.71	0.00	3.60	3.56	3.72	0.19	3.60	3.69	0.21	3.96	3.52	0.00
A person can be both a good Muslim and a loyal Australian.	3.72	4.02	0.00	3.85	3.93	4.08	0.03	3.89	4.03	0.08	4.36	3.80	0.00
Muslims find it hard to integrate into Australia.	3.40	3.33	0.21	3.40	3.37	3.23	0.03	3.38	3.29	0.11	3.22	3.39	0.01
If I saw a Muslim student being abused … I wouldn't care.	2.42	1.70	0.00	2.00	1.90	1.89	0.34	1.94	1.95	0.92	1.57	2.05	0.00

Note: Bold = $p < .05$

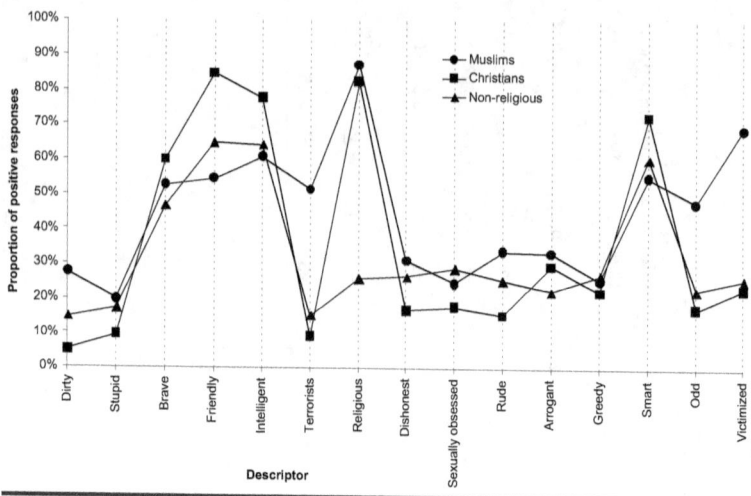

Figure 5.3
Proportion of positive responses to attributes of selected religious groups.

the two are strongly associated in a statistical sense, meaning that if one is present, the other is likely to be also.

Respondents were presented with a list of 15 attributes and asked whether or not each applied respectively to Muslims, Christians and Non-religious persons. (The latter two groups were included in order to serve as a baseline against which to compare perceptions of Muslims.) For many attributes, there was little difference in the perceptions of the religious groups, but on some the Muslims stood in sharp contrast to the others (Figure 5.3).

In order to highlight the differences between how Muslims were perceived as compared to how Christians were perceived, the difference in proportional responses were ranked.[1] Muslims were perceived (in decreasing order of importance) as more victimised, terrorists, odd, dirty, rude, dishonest, stupid, sexually obsessed, religious, arrogant and greedy than Christians; while Christians were perceived (in decreasing order of importance) as more friendly, smart, intelligent and brave than Muslims.

Data reduction

Because some of the attributes were quite similar to one another, and hence the responses to them statistically correlated, we used factor analysis to 'collapse' them into a smaller set of attributes, termed factors, with little loss of explanatory power. By reducing the amount of data this simplifies the analysis considerably and can throw light on the underlying explanatory links.

Factor analysis reduced perceptions to the following factors:

The Role of Gender, Religion and Friendship in the Perception of the 'Other'

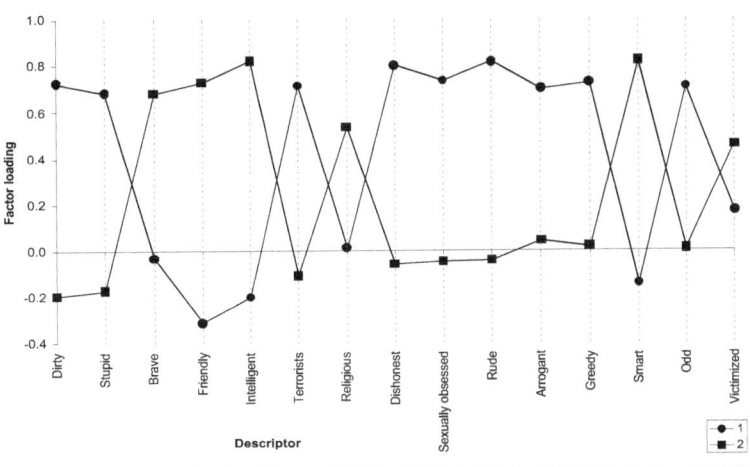

Figure 5.4
Rotated component matrix showing factor loadings: Muslims.

- Muslims: Two significant factors jointly explained 53% of observed variance.
- Christians: Three significant factors jointly explained 53% of observed variance.
- Non-religious: Three significant factors jointly explained 59% of observed variance.

Factor loadings (that is, the relative weight accorded to each perception in the factor) are shown in Figures 5.4, 5.5 and 5.6.

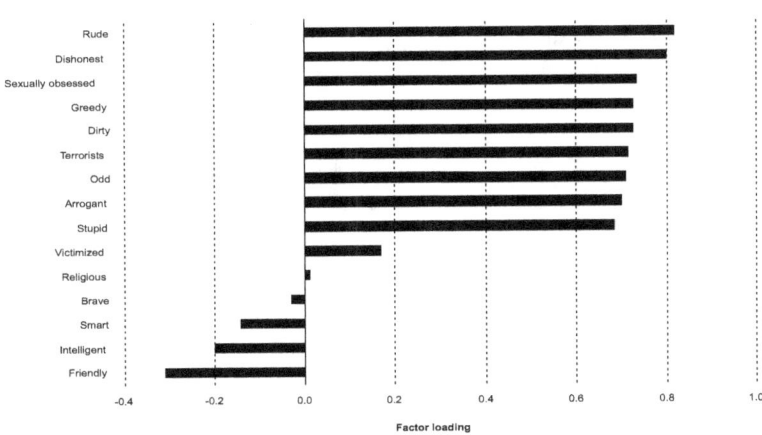

Figure 5.5
Rotated component matrix showing factor loadings: Factor 1: 'Dislikeable'.

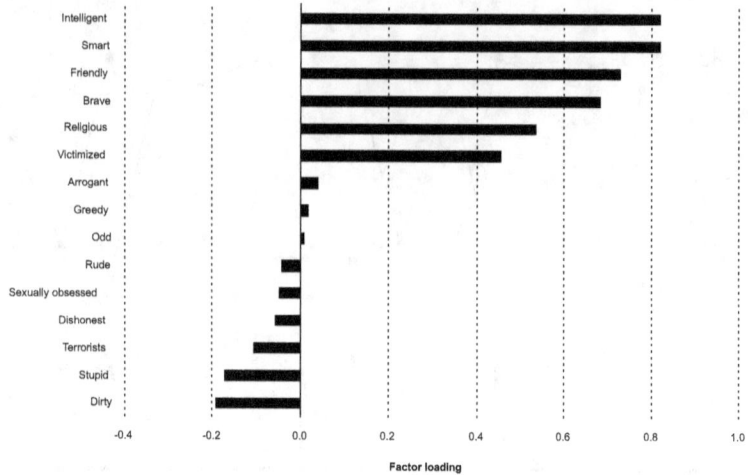

Figure 5.6
Rotated component matrix showing factor loadings: Factor 2: 'Virtuous'.
Note: Extraction method: principal component analysis.
　　　Rotation method: varimax with Kaiser normalisation.

Because the survey was concerned principally with perceptions of Muslims, the following discussion relates to them alone.

Factor 1 loads positively onto unattractive attributes (rude, dishonest, sexually obsessed, greedy, dirty, and so on); and negatively or not at all on to attractive ones (smart, intelligent, friendly etc.) or factors that are either attractive or not depending on one's subjective disposition (religious, victimised; see Figure 5.6). In the discussion we shall term it 'dislikeable'.

Factor 2 loads positively onto attractive attributes and negatively or not at all on to unattractive ones (Figure 5.6). It also loads positively on to 'religious' and 'victimised', that contribute little to Factor 1. The term used for this trait is 'virtuous' since it recognises virtues, downplays failings, and acknowledges religion — all in the context of being 'victimised'.

Conclusions

It is evident from the results that the majority of respondents are not displaying blatant prejudice. In fact, in many instance one could say that they do not seem to be displaying very much of anything, given the large number of neutral responses in the 'Attitude' section of the survey. There is a statistically insignificant minority who openly display negative attitudes toward Muslims but, as has been found in previous studies, they appear to have a general disposition of negative attitude to many things, of which cultural difference is just one.

It is always a heart-stopping moment when the data reveals a large number of neutral, non-committed, don't know, or don't care responses. And how, as researchers, are we to know which is which?

The items that drew the most 'neutral' responses were ones that asked for judgment, rather than experience. For example, 'Most religious fanatics these days are Muslims'. Very few students reported either having a Muslim friend or neighbour so anything but a 'neutral' answer would have to involve something other than personal experience. Even if the students had some contact with Muslims, they avoid labelling 'Most' with that limited experience. Thus, it appears that in this survey these students avoid the use of stereotypic labels most of the time.

When required to take a position other than that of neutrality, by being presented with a forced choice, students who had been particularly 'neutral' did not ascribe or associate negative labels with Muslims. Again, without the personal experience by which to make an informed decision, students are avoiding the use of prejudicial and stereotypic labelling.

The one result that was arguably contrary to this trend was the incidence of students associating the 'terrorist' label with Muslims. Noteworthy, a few students who had associated 'positive' labels with Muslims made this association. It is possible that the association of 'Muslim' and 'Terrorist' is an indication of subtle prejudice. If the student is associating the group 'Muslim' rather than commenting on the individual terrorist happening to be Muslim then this could be interpreted as an indication of the subtle prejudice that Pettigrew and Meertens (1997) described. Experiential learning needs to be built in to the curriculum that will facilitate the learning style preferred. Blatant racism is evident in only a minority of cases, and this seems to be coupled with a general 'negative' attitude rather than being 'Muslim specific'. Future studies should take note of this ambiguity in design and make the interpretation of the question less ambiguous.

The suggested trend, that these students are mostly reserving judgment until they have acquired evidence from personal experience, is interesting. It suggests that learning is most beneficial if it involves an experiential component. Thus, while the majority of respondents agreed that learning about Muslims would increase understanding, they rejected the idea of the school 'teaching' more. Curriculum-based comparative religion classes are hence of less benefit in fulfilling the experiential component than field trips or cultural exchange type programs that facilitate the actual meeting with, and experiencing first hand, peoples of different cultures and religions.

These students also display a distrust of information obtained by the media, both press and cinematic, which contributes to the need to rely on personal experience for obtaining information. It is not clear from this study whether this would have an impact on the role of peer groups in providing information; do peer groups proscribe the 'party line' or are peer groups formed by students who share the same experience informed opinions?

The suggestion that adolescents are now relying on personal experience to form opinions (rather than passively adopting opinions taught to them) may herald a generation that is indeed 'marching to beat of its own drum'. The corollary may be that we are seeing a generation that may acquire their sense of identity at a rate slower than previous generations. This, of course, will have many ramifications in terms of psychosocial development that are beyond the scope of this chapter.

Endnotes

1   Differences were calculated as in the following example: 69% of respondents regarded Muslims as 'victimised' as compared to 23% who regarded Christians as 'victimised', hence the difference was 23% – 69% = –46%. All differences were significant at the 5% level on paired t tests. No analogous comparison was made between Muslims and non-religious as it was considered unnecessary since perceptions of non-religious resembled perceptions of Christians.

2   Factor analysis is one of several statistical techniques collectively termed 'data reduction' methods. As the name implies, factor analysis aims to reduce large datasets with many variables to simpler datasets that capture most of the information present in the original, but with fewer variables, termed 'factors'. Each respondent is assigned a score on each factor. The numerical value of the factor score ranges between +1 (high), –1 (low) and 0 (neutral).

References

Allport, G.W. (1954). *The nature of prejudice*. Cambridge, MA: Addison-Wesley Pub. Co.

Augoustinos, M., & Reynolds, K. (Eds.) (2001). *Understanding prejudice, racism, and social conflict*. London: Sage Publications.

Berzonsky, M.D. (2004). Identity style, parental authority, and identity commitment. *Journal of Youth and Adolescence, 33,* 213–220.

Esses, V., Haddock, G., & Zanna, M.P. (1993). Values, stereotypes, and emotions as determinants of intergroup attitudes. In D.M. Mackie & D.L. Hamilton (Eds.), *Affect, cognition, and stereotyping: Interactive processes in group perception* (pp. 137–166). San Diego, CA: Academic Press.

Hunt, J.S., Seifert, A.L., Armenta, B.E., & Snowden, J.L. (2006). Stereotypes and prejudice as dynamic constructs: Reminders about the nature of intergroup bias from the hurricane katrina relief efforts. *Analyses of Social Issues and Public Policy 6*(1), 237–253.

Hutnik, N. (1991). *Ethnic minority identity: A social psychological perspective*. Oxford: Clarendon Press.

Killen, M., & McKown, C. (2005). How integrative approaches to intergroup attitudes advance the field. *Journal of Applied Developmental Psychology, 26*(6), 616–622.

Pettigrew, T.F., & Meertens, R.W. (1997). Is subtle prejudice really prejudice? *Public Opinion Quarterly, 61*(1), 54–71.

Soenens, B., Duriez, B., & Goossens, L. (2005). Social-psychological profiles of identity styles: attitudinal and social–cognitive correlates in late adolescence. *Journal of Adolescence, 28,* 107–125.

Streitmatter, J.L., & Pate, G.S. (1989). Identity status development and cognitive prejudice in early adolescents. *Journal of Early Adolescence, 9*(1–2), 142–152.

Bibliography

Asmar, C. (2001). A community on campus: Muslim students in Australian Universities. In A. Saeed & S. Akbarzadeh (Eds.), *Muslim communities in Australia* (pp. 138–160). Sydney, Australia: University of New South Wales Press.

Biggs, J. (1999). *Teaching for quality learning at university.* Buckingham, England: Society for Research and Higher Education (SRHE) and Open University Press.

Chalmers, D., & Volet, S. (1997). Common misconceptions about students from South-East Asia studying in Australia. *Higher Education Research and Development 16*(1), 87–98.

Donohoue Clyne, I. (1998). Cultural diversity and the curriculum: The Muslim experience in Australia. *European Journal of Intercultural Studies, 9*(3), 279–289.

Elliott, A., & Lemert, C. (2006). *The new individualism: The emotional costs of globalization.* London; New York: Routledge.

Inayatullah, S., & Gidley, J. (Eds.). (2000). *The university in transformation: Global perspectives on the futures of the university.* Westport, CT: Bergin & Garvey.

Jones, S., Robertson, M., & Line, M. (2000, August). International students as learners: Perceptions of students and staff at one Australian university. *HERDSA News,* 89–102.

Kember, D. (2000). Misconceptions about the learning approaches, motivation and study practices of Asian students. *Higher Education, 40,* 99–121.

Marcia, J.E. (1996). Development and validation of ego identity status. *Journal of Personality and Social Psychology, 3,* 551–558.

Martinez, C., & Sedlacek, W. (1996). *Interracial norms, behaviour and attitudes among university students.* (Research Report No. 7–82). University of Maryland, Washington, United States.

Milem, J.F. (1998). Attitude change in college students: Examining the effect of college peer groups and faculty normative groups. *Journal of Higher Education 69*(2), 117–140.

Monteith, M.J., Sherman, J.W., & Devine, P.G. (1998). Suppression as a stereotype control strategy. *Personality and Social Psychology Review, 2,* 63–82.

Nash, R.J. (2001). *Religious pluralism in the academy: Opening dialogue.* New York: Peter Lang Publishing Inc.

Nora, A., & Cabrera, A.F. (1996). The role of perceptions of prejudice and discrimination on the adjustment of minority students to college. *Journal of Higher Education 67*(2), 119–148.

Poynting, S. (2002). Bin Laden in the suburbs: attacks on Arab and Muslim Australians before and after 11 September. *Current Issues in Criminal Justice, 14*(1), 43–64

Schwartz, S.H., & Struch, N. (1989). Values, stereotypes, and intergroup antagonism. In D. Bar-Tal, C.F. Graunman, A.W. Kruglanski & W. Stroebe (Eds.), *Stereotyping and prejudice: Changing conceptions* (pp. 151–167). New York: Springer-Verlag.

Sherman, J.W. (1996). Development and mental representation of stereotypes. *Journal of Personality and Social Psychology, 70,* 1126–1141.

Sherman, J.W. (in press). On building a better process model: It's not only how many, but which ones and by which means. *Psychological Inquiry*.

Sherman, J.W., & Bessenoff, G.R. (1999). Stereotypes as source monitoring cues: On the interaction between episodic and semantic memory. *Psychological Science, 10,* 106–110.

Sherman, J.W., & Frost, L.A. (2000). On the encoding of stereotype-relevant information under cognitive load. *Personality and Social Psychology Bulletin, 26,* 26–34.

Sherman, J.W., Groom, C., Ehrenberg, K., & Klauer, K.C. (2003). Bearing false witness under pressure: Implicit and explicit components of stereotype-driven memory bias. *Social Cognition, 21,* 213–246.

Chapter 6

The Role of Australian Schools
in Educating Students About Islam and Muslims: A National Survey*

The question of knowledge of Muslims and Islam is a pressing one for Australian educational institutions in light of the reality of religious diversity and its politicisation in our society. Previous research has shown that Australians have negative perceptions of Muslims and know little about Islam, a fact often linked to discourses of moral panic emerging from the media and political spheres.

Research by Dunn (2004, 2005), using a telephone poll, shows that most Australians have little contact with Muslims and know little about Islam. Half of the respondents reported knowing little about Islam, with only a fifth claiming knowledge that was 'reasonable' or better (Dunn, 2005). Those aged 14 to 24 were the least likely to know anything about Islam and its followers (47% reported knowing nothing). Men were also more likely than women to consider themselves well informed, with tertiary-educated respondents expressing the greatest levels of knowledge.

Over two-fifths were unable to describe their perceptions of Islam. The main forms of knowledge expressed about Islam were critique of Muslims (38%) knowledge of key performances or Amal (20%), and knowledge of theology or Iman (40%). Of these, the critique of Muslims included the major stereotypes and negative views outlined in the preceding chapters — a poor form of knowledge indeed. Dunn's study showed the strong positive relationship between contact and knowledge. His research also shows the reduction of 'Islamophobia through both contact with Muslims and knowledge of Islam.

---

*This chapter was co-authored with Joel Windle (2007). Reprinted with permission from the *Australian Quarterley*.

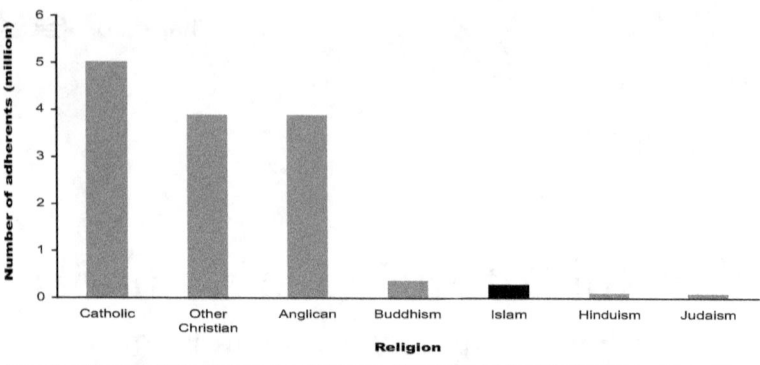

Figure 6.1
Religious affiliation: Population in 2001.

The relative recent establishment of the Muslim community in Australia, and the lack of contact many Australians have with Muslims may have exacerbated the problem. Indeed, schools have sought to address the issue of tension with new arrivals since the children of postwar migrants entered the education system in large numbers in the 1970s. Multiculturalism has been the official approach for nearly 30 years, with its implementation focused on inclusive styles rather than new curriculum content. This chapter analyses the attitudes and knowledge of non-Muslim Australian students and their views on the contribution of their schools to this knowledge base. It draws on a recent nationwide survey of Year 11 students. First, an outline of the Muslim community in Australia and attitudes towards it is described, before discussing the posture of schools in relation to cultural diversity. A number of theoretical orientations supporting the study are discussed before the presentation of results.

Background

Muslims in Australia

The Muslim community, although still small (Figure 6.1), is one of the fastest growing religious communities in Australia. It nearly doubled in the 5 years from 1996 to 2001, growing from 210,000 to 282,000 and showed an overall rise of 91% in the last decade. Australian Muslims are ethnically diverse and come from a wide range of backgrounds and cultures. Some 35% of Australian Muslims were born in Australia, and the rest have migrated to Australia from over 70 different countries, including Lebanon, Turkey, Indonesia and Bosnia-Herzegovina (Dunn, 2004).

There are almost 100 mosques and over 25 Muslim schools in Australia (although these schools cater to less than 1% of Muslim students; Donohoue

Clyne, 2001). Reflecting the increasing recognition in Australia of the Islamic faith, Islam now is the second-largest religion in Australia, after Christianity and Buddhism. It is possible that it could move into second place in the coming decade.

Attitudes towards Islam and Muslims in Australia

In Australia, attitudes towards Islam cannot be separated from the history of migration, the social and ethnic composition of Muslim communities, and the politics of global conflict. In this context, racism, particularly in the form of cultural racism, denotes here disapproval of morality. Such negative views are widespread in the media, academic and government texts (Goodall & Jakubowicz, 1994; Human Rights and Equal Opportunity Commission, 2004).

Internationally, negative stereotyping of Islam and Muslims has been linked to the first Gulf War, the war in Iraq, September 11, and other terrorist attacks. Poynting (2002) notes the increase in assaults on people of 'Middle Eastern appearance', women wearing the hijab and men wearing 'Islamic garb' after the outbreak of the first Gulf War. Women and girls emerged as the most frequent targets. At the same time there was an increase in arson, vandalism and threats of assault directed towards the newly discovered 'enemy within'. Poynting points to the role of tabloid media, in particular talkback radio, in whipping up racist sentiments at this time, and following September 11 (with a similar increase in racist incidents).

A discourse joining Arab–Muslim–Terrorist worked to join the terms 'Gang-Rapist', 'Arab–Muslim' by the same means, particularly in Sydney, following a series of sexual assaults in Bankstown (Poynting, 2002). Concern about Middle-Eastern asylum seekers, particularly at the time of the 2001 federal election campaign, contributed to distrust, fear, and the emergence of racist discourses. In these instances, politicians join with powerful talkback personalities and columnists to create a sense of panic. This process highlights the fact that the media is primary source of information about Islam and what it stands for (Brasted, 2001), rather than the Koran or direct contact. The economic, historical and religious diversity of some 60 Muslim countries are rarely presented in the media.

These patterns of representation and attack were felt in schools, with the emergence of 'SOB' ('straight off the boat') as a playground insult. The Australian Arabic Council's Racism Register records a school in south-eastern Melbourne being graffitied with 'die Muslim scum' and threats being made at school to Muslim students (Australian Arabic Council, 2001). At university level too, students feel frustration at their teachers' lack of knowledge of Islam and reliance on media representations (Asmar, 2001; Speck, 1997).

By contrast, in an earlier period, Bullivant (1987, 1988) brushed off concerns about discrimination faced by migrant background students by postulating a migrant 'success ethic'. Cahill and Gundert (1996) similarly concluded from a large-scale study that 'the general climate of Australian schools is healthy and positive for minority Australian students with cultural, religious and racial backgrounds different to those of mainstream Australian students. This is despite a perception of hostility from peers and teachers expressed by some migrant background students (particularly girls), and teacher concerns about the participation of girls in activities and Ramadan. Other reports have suggested school is the location for much discrimination on the basis of ethnicity (Human Rights and Equal Opportunity Commission, 2004). A study of Victorian schools (Ata & Batrouney, 1989) showed that the type of school attended correlated with the degree of stereotyping. Private school students were more likely to accept negative stereotypes of Muslims and Arabs. The study involved the application of words such as 'rude', 'rich', 'intelligent', 'aggressive', 'lecherous' and 'primitive'.

Attitudes in Australian schools

Australian schools have not been the battleground for debates about Islam and Muslims in the way they have been in France, where school is understood as supporting a universal national identity to the exclusion of all others (Windle, 2004). The Australian Government's adoption of multiculturalism after the Galbally report (Galbally, 1978) recommended the management of ethnic identity as a policy goal in Australian schools. That same year saw the establishment of the Committee on Multicultural Education by the Commonwealth, followed by funding for the now defunct Commonwealth Multicultural Education Program (MEP).

More recently, equal opportunity legislation and the development of antiracism resources such as 'Racism No Way' (Department of Education and Training, 2000) has provided schools with further impetus to deal with discrimination. Teacher training and guidelines from education authorities provide advice on managing student diversity in schools through sensitive and inclusive approaches to pedagogy and curriculum.

It is beyond the scope of this chapter to review all curricula on managing cultural diversity or on Islam and Muslims, however, I will draw on some Victorian examples to illustrate the general policy of Australian schools.

In Victoria, the Department of Education provides no information or resources specific to Islam or Muslims. Under the rubric of cultural and linguistic diversity it provides a general set of guidelines, with resources for teachers (Department of Education Employment and Training, 2001) together with an overarching multicultural policy document (Department of Education, 1997). Cultural diversity is operationalised primarily as linguistic diversity, with no reference to religion.

The Victorian guidelines seek to promote the valuing of diverse perspectives in the classroom, and intercultural communication. Knowledge of particular backgrounds is mentioned as a goal, but does not form part of the approaches outlined (Department of Education, 1997) and does not appear as something that schools can offer students. This is in contrast to the emphasis on in-depth understanding of cultural norms and practices (Donohoue Clyne, 2000) and active critical interrogation (Kalantzis & Cope, 1984) that is placed at the centre of intercultural communication by some. A reactive approach to dealing with perspectives and bias means that the content and extent of knowledge gained in the classroom will be dependent on the range of concerns, if any, students express on questions relating to religion, identity and their relationship to world events. This approach is illustrated in the advice provided by the Department of Education on dealing with international tensions:

> Students bring with them into the classroom many preconceptions and assumptions that influence their views about how the world works. Classroom activities may therefore impact differently on individuals according to their cultural, religious and linguistic backgrounds. All schools need to strive to create learning environments that encourage the questioning of stereotypes, and the rejection of bias, bigotry and prejudice.

Where controversial and worrying issues are involved, storytelling, drama and creative arts activities have long been recognised as useful vehicles for allowing students to air their concerns in ways that provide opportunities for further discussion. For older students, the use of structured discussion techniques can also assist in opening up contentious issues without requiring a commitment to a particular point of view (Department of Education, 2003).

Many teachers do indeed take the opportunity to discuss Islam when it is raised by students, as an incidental and tangential part of teaching. Beyond multiculturalism as an approach, there appear to be few places in the curriculum where students are taught about Muslims and Islam. The main contexts in the secondary setting in Victoria are far removed from either the Muslim community in Australia or the wider world: the Crusades, the Ottoman empire, or classical Islamic architecture. Ata and Batrouney's study (1989) found that the absence of both comprehensive relevant curriculum material and teachers with insight into both cultures was a primary factor behind stereotyping.

The comparative lack of curriculum, and indeed Islamic studies in tertiary education, is all the more surprising given the mounting economic, professional and educational exchange between Australia and Muslim countries. For example, in 2003 Australia exported A$7 billion worth of goods to the Gulf region and Middle East, Indonesia and Malaysia. An estimated total of 20,000 Australian teachers, nurses, expatriates and other professionals are working in those regions. Likewise, the number of full fee paying Muslim students from overseas is at an all time high. (Insight editorial, 2008).

There have been recent calls for schools to take an active role in managing a 'Muslim problem' in Australia. The government-sponsored 'National Muslim Youth Summit' identified education and schools as central to resolving 'the perceived conflict between Muslim and Australian identity' (Muslim Community Reference Group, 2006, p. 36). However, together with the Muslim Community Reference group, it proceeded on the basis that Muslims need to work to resolve problems with Muslims — including the discrimination they face from broader society. The 'victim' remains at the centre of resolution of the problem for which it bears the burden. In its response to the reference group's proposals, the Federal government adopts a similar perspective, aiming to support young Muslims to develop strategies to cope with their own discrimination and vilification (Muslim Community Reference Group, 2006).

Theories of cultural conflict and harmony

Edward Sa'id considers negative views of Muslims and Islam arise from the history of colonialism, with 'orientalism' (the tradition of romanticised and reductionist representations in Western culture) serving an instrumental purpose (Said, 1995). This cultural construction extends to the postcolonial period and facilitates military adventurism and economic domination (Said, 1981).

Negative stereotypes do indeed appear to remain widespread in 'the West'. Polling in over 50 countries revealed that Westerners view Muslims as fanatical, violent, and intolerant. Meanwhile Muslims perceive Westerners to be selfish, immoral, and greedy, as well as violent and fanatical. Each group viewed the other as being disrespectful towards women (Pew Research Centre, 2006.

An alternative theory emerging from the pioneering work of the Chicago school posits negative views of any new group in a society as a source of anxiety that dissipates over time, with eventual incorporation into broader society (Park, Burgess, & McKenzie, 1925). As Muslims are a relatively 'new' group in Australia, this thesis suggests that with the cycle of cultural assimilation of the second generation, other, newer arrivals will instead bear the brunt of discrimination.

More recent research suggests that such boundaries may not always be temporary and that conflict between groups is the product of threats to group positioning and the protection of acquired privilege (Bobo & Hutchings, 1996). Those who see themselves in competition with Muslims (over scarce jobs, education, housing), that is to say, those at the bottom of the class structure where most Muslims are also located, are most likely to be threatened and to feel antipathy towards them according to this thesis. Support is provided by the concentration of political parties expressing ethnocentrist and antimigrant views in low socioeconomic status areas (Davis & Stimson, 1988). A neo-Marxist angle on this view is summarised by Dunn (2001, p. 30): 'Racism is a political means of dividing the working class ... segregation, and racism generally, are therefore seen as manifestations of interworking class competition encouraged by the elite'.

Dunn (2005) suggests that social contact with, and knowledge about Muslims can have a powerful positive effect, but the group competition thesis suggests that other factors may inhibit this process. The contact thesis suggests that prejudice is likely to be greater in areas with low levels of ethnic diversity, such as rural Australia — again supported by voting patterns for One Nation (Davis & Stimson, 1988) and levels of ethnocentric attitudes (Dunn, 2001).

The negative image of Muslim communities as a threat to mainstream civic Australian life may have worked its way to a certain degree into the consciousness of students. This can be expected to be greater among those in a monocultural setting and who have little contact with Muslims. Alternatively, the long-standing policy of multiculturalism in Australian schools may counter such tendencies.

Methods

Participants

The participants were 1000 students at 20 secondary schools around Australia (excluding the Northern Territory and Western Australia)[1] who were administered a full-length survey[2] examining general attitudes towards Muslims and Islam. Participating students were from Years 10–12. Secondary schools of Muslim or Jewish affiliation were not approached for this survey, nor were Muslim or Jewish students. It is anticipated that differences will exist within these groups towards Muslims and Islam, and it is intended to study these groups in subsequent surveys. Primarily, the responses of Muslim and Jewish students were likely to be unrepresentative of most Australians. The particular characteristics of our sample are presented in detail in Chapter 3.

Procedure

In each selected school, the survey was administered to all eligible students present on the day of the survey. Schools were requested to survey Year 11 students, as they were considered mature enough to give informed answers, yet unencumbered by Year 12 exams. Even so, many schools chose to administer the survey to Year 12 and Year 10 students. This was an unplanned bonus, as it allowed us to test the impact of another demographic variable. Schools were selected by first seeking permission from the following school agencies in the relevant States and Territory: State Government Departments dealing with education, Catholic Education Offices, and Independent School Councils.

Aims

The primary aim of the study was to identify, analyse and interpret the knowledge, values, and attitudes of Year 11 students with respect to Islam and the Muslim communities. The goal of this chapter is to explore the links between students' knowledge and views and the attitude adopted by schools, and how these influence representations of Islam and Muslims.

Results

Students' knowledge of Muslims and Islam

The survey revealed a great lack of knowledge of Islam: on all questions about half the sample recorded a 'don't know' response (Figure 6.2). It emerges that most students are ignorant about who Muslims are, where they live and what they believe. The proportion of correct responses varied from a high of 49% for 'Some Palestinians are Christian', to a low of 6% for 'Iran is an Arab country'. Given the important role of conflict in the Middle East in discourses shaping

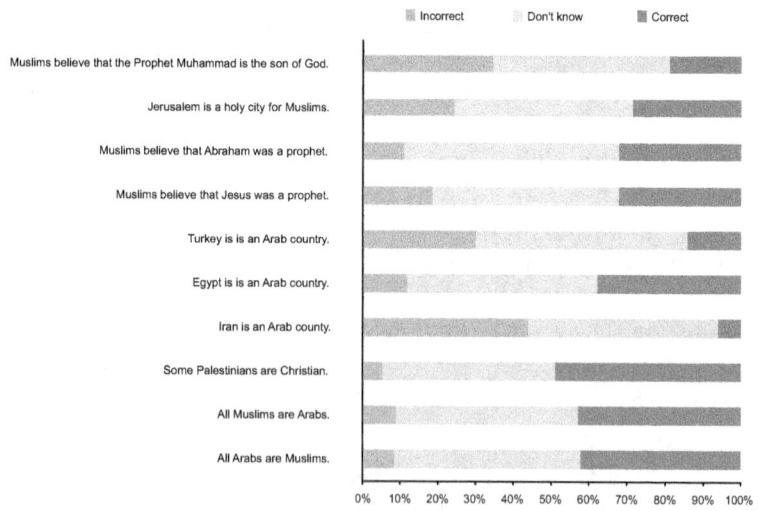

Figure 6.2
Proportion of correct and incorrect responses.

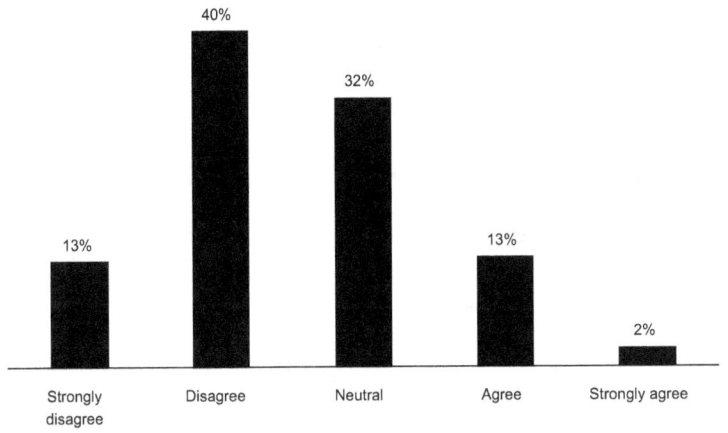

Figure 6.3
'The image of Muslims is as good as other migrant groups in Australia.'

views on Islam and Muslims, it is worrying that students are forming their perceptions without much actual knowledge. These levels of ignorance among school students confirm Dunn's findings for the population at large, suggesting that current schooling is not a major source of information for students, or at least provides no more information than it did to previous generations.

Perceptions of Muslims in Australia
While most participants indicated good feelings towards and acceptance of Muslims, they are conscious of their negative image (Figure 6.3). A clear demarcation of the perceived image of Muslims compared to other migrant groups is revealed. The results show a total of 53% disagreed that the image of Muslims is as good as other migrant groups; only 13% agreed and 2% agreed strongly. No significant differences emerge between students who have contact with Muslims and those who don't, suggesting that students gain this common perception from beyond their immediate circle, suggesting the importance of national discourses. On average, boys are more likely to think that Muslims have a negative image than girls (see Table 6.1), which is consistent with their more pessimistic view on the ability of school to help students of different backgrounds get along.

It follows from the poor image attributed to Muslims that 38% of students agree that Muslims find it hard to integrate into Australia (Figure 6.4). The proportion of students who believe Muslims find it hard to integrate is less than the 53% who consider them to have an image problem, suggesting that students feel that Muslims face more obstacles than negative representations.

Table 6.1
Means and Significance Levels by Group and Question

	Sex			Religion				Having Muslim Neighbours		
	Male	Female	Sig.	Catholic	Other Christian	Not religious	Sig.	Yes	No	Sig.
The image of Muslims is as good as other migrant groups in Australia	-0.55	-0.42	0.00	-0.48	-0.53	-0.45	0.46	-0.47	-0.48	0.96
Muslims find it hard to integrate into Australia	0.04	0.33	0.21	0.40	0.37	0.23	0.03	0.40	0.35	0.64
I have learnt a lot about Muslims at this school.	-0.61	-0.59	0.87	-0.54	-0.68	-0.61	0.21	-0.48	-0.61	0.39
Since being at this school I understand Muslims better.	-0.39	-0.44	0.52	-0.34	-0.50	-0.47	0.10	-0.43	-0.42	0.99
This school helps people of different cultures to get along better.	0.25	0.53	0.00**	0.40	0.48	0.45	0.57	0.52	0.43	0.54
Australian schools should teach more about Muslims.	-0.55	-0.09	0.00**	-0.31	-0.35	-0.03	0.00	-0.14	-0.25	0.46

Note: The mean is situated on a five point Likert scale with -2 being the most negative response (strongly disagree) and +2 being the most positive (strongly agree).

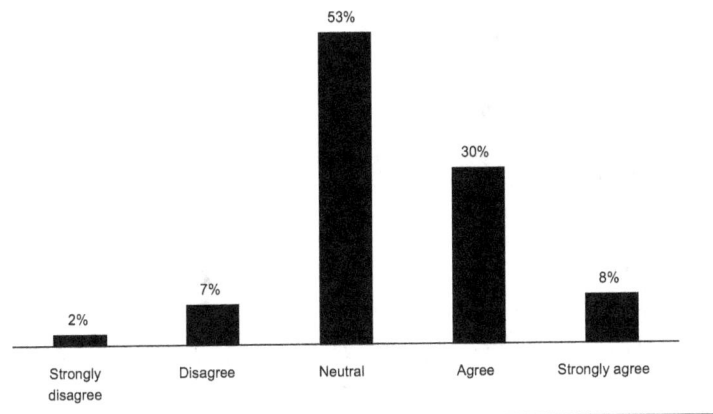

Figure 6.4
'Muslims find it hard to integrate into Australia.'

Those students who have Muslim friends view this integration as significantly less difficult, suggesting that the realities may not be as dark as the media portrait painted.

The contribution of schools

In light of the students' lack of knowledge, but also their recognition of the difficulties faced by Muslims, the role of schools is of central importance. Students do not feel that schools are doing a good job informing them (Figure 6.5). A clear majority do not feel they have learned a lot about Muslims at their school, with over a fifth strongly disagreeing with the proposition (a figure that exceeds the proportion of positive responses). A mere 2% felt they could give the most positive response. The small response (16%) by those who learned a lot about Muslims at their school is understandable. Educational textbooks and special units on this subject matter are largely absent from school curricula. Library textbooks on this subject are rare, inappropriate, theological, orientalist, old, or translated poorly.

Similarly, a large percentage of respondents (49%) disagreed that they understand Muslims better since being at their school; 22% agreed (Figure 6.6). The absence of Muslim students from a large number of private schools and regional Australia may have contributed to the direction of responses in this figure, although having Muslim friends does not make a significant difference. Information from peers and social experiences may nonetheless account for the slightly more positive responses to this item. As discussed earlier, it likely that references to Muslims have been made but in a casual manner, confined to historical events.

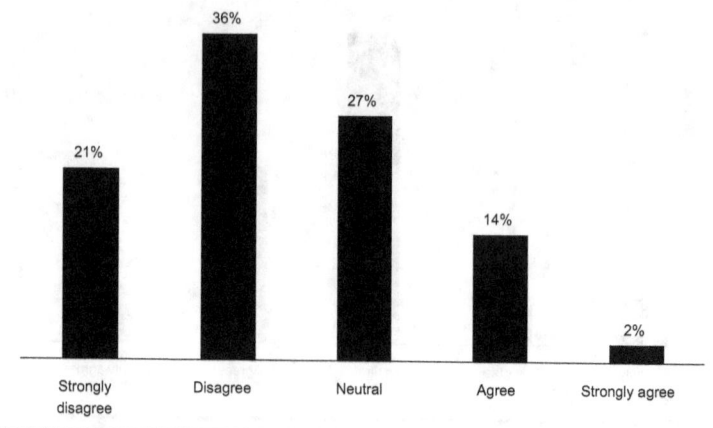

Figure 6.5
'I have learned a lot about Muslims at this school.'

One of the key goals of knowledge and understanding of others is promoting cultural harmony. However, knowledge and understanding of Muslims does not appear to be a precondition for a belief that schools promote cultural harmony. Findings shown in Figure 6.7 reveal that the largest percentage of respondents (53%) agree that their school helps people of different cultures to get along better. Clearly this percentage is not to be viewed as incompatible with the responses in the previous figure, namely that only 22% understand Muslims better at their schools. Some schools were found to have students from different religious and cultural background but not Muslim, which may explain

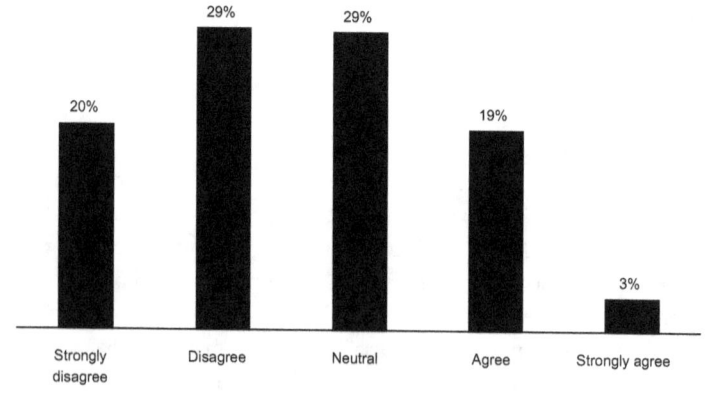

Figure 6.6
'Since being at this school I understand Muslims better.'

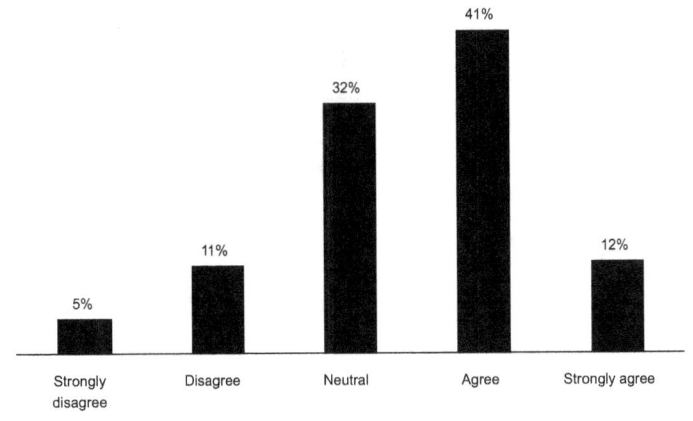

Figure 6.7
'This school helps people of different cultures to get along better.'

this positive outlook that is more marked among students with one or both parents born overseas.

Another explanation may be that students consider the provision of a non-conflictual social environment and the display of inclusive values may be sufficient to fulfil this goal. This would fit with the policy orientations of multiculturalism. Boys are more pessimistic on average about their school's helpfulness than girls; this matches with their stronger perception that Muslims are negatively viewed. Students with Muslim friends were also significantly more negative than others, indicating that cultural inclusiveness may not always extend to this group.

The picture that emerges is somewhat paradoxical if we accept that knowledge and understanding are valuable tools to combat negative images and difficulties in finding acceptance. Students know little and learn little from school, but consider that schools are to some extent successful in countering acknowledged difficulties faced by Muslims. Do they also believe that schools should teach more about Muslims, or are they happy with the way things are?

What should schools be doing?

When asked whether Australian schools should teach more about Muslims, more respondents disagreed (40%) with the statement than agreed (25%) (Figure 6.8). Thirty-five per cent expressed no opinion. A quarter of respondents have acknowledged that more teaching about Muslims in Australian schools is needed, but the level of complacency is disturbing (Figure 6.8).

There was disagreement between groups regarding this proposition, with Christian students being significantly less favourable than those with no stated

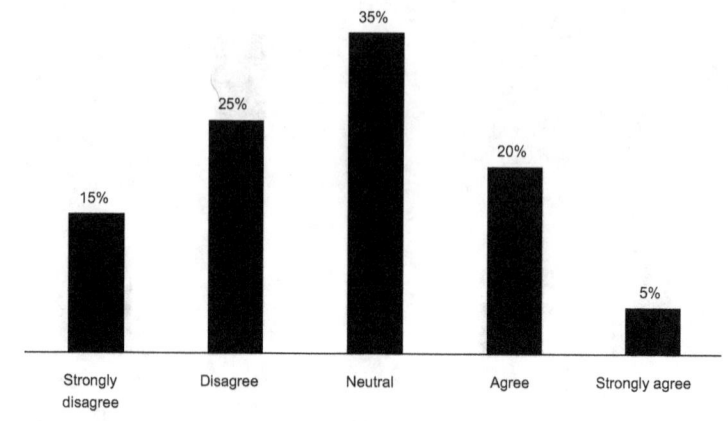

Figure 6.8
'Australian schools should teach more about Muslims.'

religion. Boys were also less interested than girls in learning more about Muslims. Surprisingly, students with Muslim friends were also less likely than those without to consider it necessary to increase teaching about Muslims (see Table 3.1).

Discussion and Implications

From these data is appears that non-Muslim students do not perceive their own ignorance as the main difficulty facing Muslims in society, and further that the promotion of cultural harmony in schools does not necessarily work through increasing knowledge. The paradoxical disconnection of knowledge from the difficulties students see facing Muslims points to particular challenges for schools, where knowledge is, after all, the core business.

Agreement on the difficulties facing Muslims and some widespread misconceptions support the thesis of an all powerful media discourse, supported by political and economic interests. It is also consistent with the social competition thesis. The benefit of personal contact is supported by the distinctive views of students with Muslim friends, although having Muslim neighbours does not appear to make a significant difference to responses.

Given the widespread discourses promulgating negative stereotypes, it is clear that schools need to actively engage with these. Frameworks in Queensland and Tasmania make use of critical literacy approaches that could be a useful rubric for this, while some school texts provide practical approaches to representations of ethnicity in the media (Dunscombe, 2004). An important step is to break down the image of the monolith of the Arab–Muslim to appreciate the diversity and specificities of the full range of faiths espoused by Arabs, and in majority Arab countries, as well as ethnic and religious diversity among Muslims. A similarly monolithic vision of 'Christian Culture' in Australia is also an obstacle to be addressed within the Muslim community (Ata, 2004). It is worth considering the contribution that outsiders to the education bureaucracy can make, particularly those from the Muslim community, to the development of policies, curriculum materials and pedagogical practices.

Current multicultural policies and student responses alike appear to de-emphasise knowledge as a means to understanding and cultural harmony, and this appears as a major problem heading into the future.

The broader literature at tertiary level indicates that knowledge of, and experience with, minority groups at university offers great potential for change on both intellectual and personal levels. Multicultural courses in particular offer a forum to induce personal change. The results show overwhelming that there are several positive outcomes attained by students acquiring knowledge from an intercultural relations course, as compared to students enrolled in a control group.

Attitudes of students in the intercultural relations courses were significantly higher in multicultural ideology, and significantly more tolerant of different cultures. Another form of personal growth presumed to be the byproduct of multicultural education is an increased self-esteem. These findings are encouraging because they indicate that topics focusing on ethnic diversity can have a positive impact on student attitudes toward multicultural ideology, ethnic tolerance, and self-worth.

The findings presented here point to a number of challenges:

- *Curriculum*: educate students about Australian society and the world more completely. What kind of knowledge is most useful here? Religious, historical, social content — where in the curriculum should it be located?
- *Intercultural relations*: schools have a responsibility to address or redress prejudiced social attitudes through knowledge (not just the social environment they provide).
- *Active citizenship*: students need to be equipped to engage in political and social discussion in an informed way, particularly in global context. This includes an understanding of how stereotypes emerge and the conditions and sources of religious and/or social conflict.

Acknowledgment

The author wishes to acknowledge the contribution of Joel Windle in cowriting this chapter. This research first appeared in *Australian Quarterly*.

Endnotes

1 These locations were excluded as it would have been costly to survey them for logistical reasons (in any case it was thought they would not contribute to survey accuracy as there was no reason to suppose their responses would differ from those in other states).

2 A pilot study was conducted at nine schools with 552 students, and a short form survey was conducted at 13 schools with 682 students.

References

Ata, A. & Windle, J. (2007). The role of Australian schools in educating students about Islam and Muslims. *Australian Quarterly, 79*(6), 19–27.

Akbarzadeh, & A. Saeed (Eds.). (2001). *Muslim communities in Australia*. Sydney, Australia: UNSW Press.

Asmar, C. (2001). A community on campus: Muslim students in Australian universities. In S. Akbarzadeh & A. Saeed (Eds.), *Muslim communities in Australia* (pp. 139–160). Sydney, Australia: UNSW Press.

Brasted, H. (2001). Contested representations in historical perspective: Images of Islam and the Australian press 1950–2000. In S. Akbarzadeh & A. Saeed (Eds.), *Muslim communities in Australia*. Sydney, Australia: UNSW Press.

Bullivant, B.M. (1987). *The ethnic encounter in the secondary school: Ethnocultural reproduction and resistance: Theory and case studies*. London; New York: Falmer Press.

Bullivant, B. M. (1988). The ethnic success ethic challenges conventional wisdom about immigrant disadvantages in Australia. *Australian Journal of Education, 32*(2), 223–243.

Cahill, D., & Gundert, A. (1996). *Immigration and schooling in the 1990s*. Canberra, Australia: Australian Government Publishing Service.

Davis, R., & Stimson, R. (1988). Disillusionment and disenchantment at the fringe: Explaining the geography of the one nation party vote at the Queensland election. *People and Place, 6*, 69–82.

Department of Education and Training. (2000). *Racism. No way: Anti-racism education for Australian schools*. Retrieved January 17, 2006, from http://www.racismnoway.com.au/

Dunn, K. (2001). The geography of racism in NSW: A theoretical exploration and some preliminary findings from the mid 1990s. *The Australian Geographer, 32*(1), 29–44.

Dunn, K. (2004). Islam in Australia: Contesting the discourse of absence. *The Australian Geographer, 53*(3), 333–353.

Dunn, K. (2005). Australian public knowledge of Islam. *Studia Islamika: Indonesian Journal for Islamic Studies, 12*(1), 1–32.

Dunscombe, R. (2004). *Heinemann media 1. Units 1 & 2*. Melbourne, Australia: Heinemann.

Goodall, H., & Jakubowicz, A. (1994). *Racism, ethnicity and the media*. Sydney, Australia: Allen & Unwin.

Human Rights and Equal Opportunity Commission. (2004). *Ismau listen: National consultations on eliminating prejudice against Arab and Muslim Australians*. Sydney, Australia: Author.

Insight editorial. (2008, July 26). *The Age*, p. 8.

Kalantzis, M., & Cope, B. (1984). Multiculturalism and education policy. In G. Bottomley & M. M. De Lepervanche (Eds.), *Ethnicity, class and gender in Australia*. Sydney, Australia: George Allen and Unwin.

Omar, W., Hughes, P.J., & Allen, K. (1996). *The Muslims in Australia*. Canberra, Australia: Bureau of Immigration Multicultural and Population Research.

Park, R.E., Burgess, E.W., & McKenzie, R.D. (1925). *The city*. Chicago: University of Chicago Press.

Pew Research Centre. (2006). *Conflicting views in a divided world*. Washington, DC: The Pew Global Attitudes Project.

Poynting, S. (2002). Bin Laden in the suburbs: Attacks on Arab and Muslim Australians before and after 11 September. *Current Issues in Criminal Justice, 14*(1), 43–64.

Rieder, J. (1985). *Canarsie: The Jews and Italians of Brooklyn against liberalism*. Cambridge, Massachusetts: Harvard University Press.

Said, E. (1981). *Covering Islam: How the media and the experts determine how we see the rest of the world*. New York: Pantheon Books.

Said, E. (1995). *Orientalism*. New York: Penguin.

Windle, J. (2004). Schooling, symbolism and social power: The hijab in Republican France. *Australian Educational Researcher, 31*(1), 95–112.

Bibliography

Ata, A. (2005). Beyond the stereotypes. *Quadrant, 413*(49), 19–26.

Ata, A. (2006a). Demonising Australia's Christian and Muslim Arabs in Cartoons. *Compass, 40*(summer), 31–34.

Ata, A. (2006b). Observing different faiths, learning about ourselves: Practice with inter-married Muslims and Christians. *Australian Social Work, 59*(3), 250–264.

Ata, A. (2006, November 17). Lost in translation: Australia's top cleric. *Australian E Journal of Social Debate*, 1–3.

Department of Education Employment and Training. (2001). *Guidelines for managing cultural and linguistic diversity in schools*. Melbourne: State of Victoria.

Donohoue Clyne, I. (2001). Educating Muslim children in Australia. In S. Akbarzadeh & A. Saeed (Eds.), *Muslim communities in Australia*. Sydney, Australia: UNSW Press.

Simkin, K., & Gauci, E. (1992). Ethnic diversity and multicultural education. In R.J. Burns & A.R. Welch (Eds.), *Contemporary perspectives in comparative education*. New York: Garland Publications.

Chapter 7

Social Distance From Muslims
A National Survey

Social distance is a notion by which individuals are able to recognise how others are both similar and different from them in forming social attitudes. The hypothesis is usually introduced to measure individual attitudes in the context of race relations. It measures the way individuals stereotype members of other minority groups. The hypothesis makes the following assumption: the more experience a person shares with members of other groups the more positive attitudes are formed towards them. The Social Distance or Contact Hypothesis holds that experience can assist in correcting false assumptions and prejudices towards other minority groups. It also holds that shared experience with others results in a sense of connection with them.

The importance of the theory is that contact with specific members of an outgroup are not limited to a specific situation and the immediate outgroup members, but instead said to generalise to the outgroup, thereby reducing prejudice to the outgroup as a whole. Allport (1954) stressed that for contact to have the desired impact on prejudicial attitudes the conditions of equal status, common goals, intergroup cooperation and support of the authorities, law, or custom were key conditions. However, there have often been conflicting and mixed results regarding these conditions. This provides strong support to the major premise of the contact hypothesis that mere contact with members of another group is a powerful force in the reduction of prejudice. (Hewstone, 1990; Pettigrew, 2006).

American, British and Australian researchers vary in their definition about what constitutes contact, often leading to support the opposite generalisation. For example, Pettigrew & Tropp (2006) believe contact is face-to-face interaction; however, other studies define contact in more relaxed ways (e.g., intergroup proximity). Some forms of contact would be expected to satisfy Allport's conditions more than others, and indeed cross-group friendships are likely to encompass aspects of equal status, cooperation and common goals. As a result it is not uncommon to encounter findings of forms of contact, for example into select minorities such as single working mothers and divorcees, to be asymmetrical and not consistent.

Given this emphasis it is also reasonable to assume that variations in social and cultural (i.e., normative) context may lead to some variation in the relationship between these broader factors and their effect on the efficacy of intergroup contact.

Respondents were presented with 12 statements concerning desired social distance), and asked to rate their agreement on a 5-point scale from *Strongly agree* through *Neutral* to *Strongly disagree*. The statements formed graduated triads. Half concerned the social distance of the respondent and half of the respondent's parents; and half concerned the social distance from 'another [unspecified] race' and half from Muslims, as shown in Table 7.1.

Method

An initial group of 1,000 students from 20 secondary schools around Australia were administered a full-length survey examining general attitudes towards Muslims and Islam in February to July 2006. The Northern Territory and the state of Western Australia were excluded for logistical reasons; there was no reason to suppose their responses would differ from those in other states. The current research was part of a larger study examining the attitudes of non-Muslim and non-Jewish secondary schools students towards Muslims and

Table 7.1
Social Distance from 'Another Race'

Social distance from ...	
'Another race'	Muslims
Respondent	
• I would enjoy having a close friend of another race	• I would enjoy having a close Muslim friend
• I would go out with someone of another race	• I would go out with a Muslim
• I would marry someone of another race.	• I would marry a Muslim
Parents	
• My parents would be happy if I had a close friend of another race	• My parents would be happy if I had a close Muslim friend
• My parents would be happy if I went out with someone of another race	• My parents would be happy if I went out with a Muslim
• My parents would be happy if I married someone of another race.	• My parents would be happy if I married a Muslim

Islam (Ata, 2007). Schools were selected by seeking permission from education departments, Catholic Education Offices, and Independent School Councils. Participating schools were either Christian (13 Catholic, 1 'other' Christian school) or non-religious (3 independent, 2 government schools). Participating students were from Years 10 to 12, where Year 10 pupils are aged 14 to 16 years; Year 11, aged 15 to 17 years; and Year 12 aged 16 to 18 years.

Respondents were presented with 12 statements concerning desired social distance, and asked to rate their agreement on a 5-point scale from *Strongly agree* through *Neutral* to *Strongly disagree*. The statements formed graduated triads. Half concerned the social distance of the respondent and half of the respondent's parents; and half concerned the social distance from 'another [unspecified] race' and half from Muslims, as shown below.

Social distance from 'another race' was measured in order to serve as a baseline against which to compare social distance from Muslims. Social distance of parents was measured in order to determine its statistical association with that of respondents.

Results and Discussion

Social distance from 'another race'

Respondents overwhelmingly agreed with all three statements (see Figure 7.1). For instance, nearly three-quarters agreed with 'I would enjoy having a close

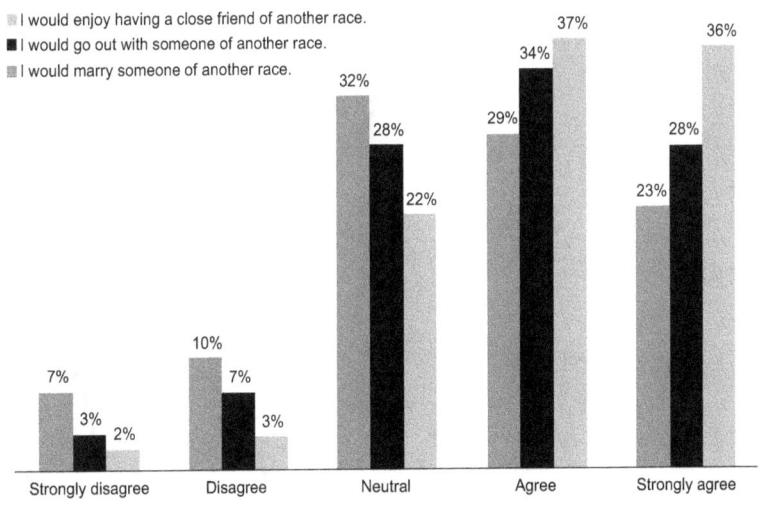

Figure 7.1
Proportion of respondents, by social distance of self from 'another race'.
Note: N = 993, 993 and 991 respectively.

friend of another race', and just over half with 'I would marry someone of another race.' Agreement was strongest for the statement indicating least social proximity, and weakest (but still overwhelmingly positive) for that indicating most social proximity. This is as expected; it would be irrational for a respondent to agree more strongly with the more strongly worded statement.

Social distance from Muslims

Respondents were less likely to agree with the statements relating to 'Muslims' than with the corresponding statements relating to 'another race' (Figure 7.2); and the greater the social proximity indicated by the statement, the greater the disparity. For example, about three-quarters agreed with 'I would enjoy having a close friend of another race', but only about half with 'I would enjoy having a close Muslim friend'; and while about half agreed with 'I would marry someone of another race', only a fifth did so for 'I would marry a Muslim'.

Comparison

It is common to desire a certain social distance from others, the more so if they are of another race. But do respondents want more or less social distance from Muslims as compared to persons of another race?

There was significant difference between the desired social difference from Muslims and that from persons of 'another race', and the greater the social proximity indicated by the statement, the greater the disparity. The difference

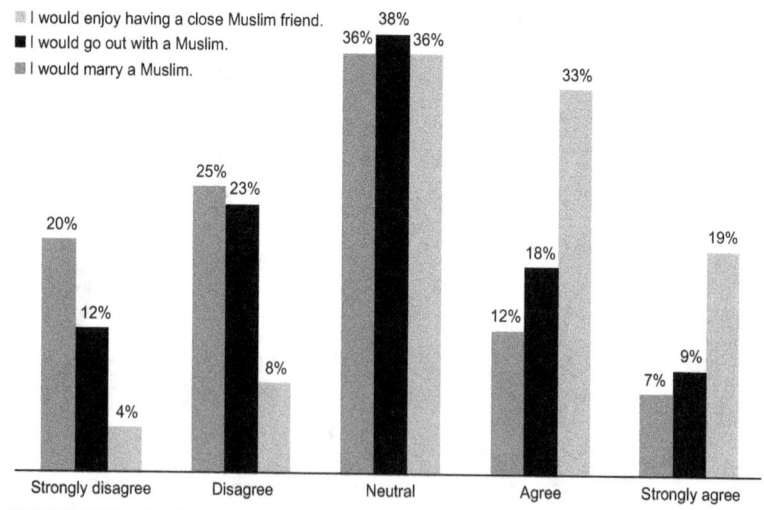

Figure 7.2
Proportion of respondents, by social distance of self from Muslims.
Note: *N* = 994, 994 and 991 respectively.

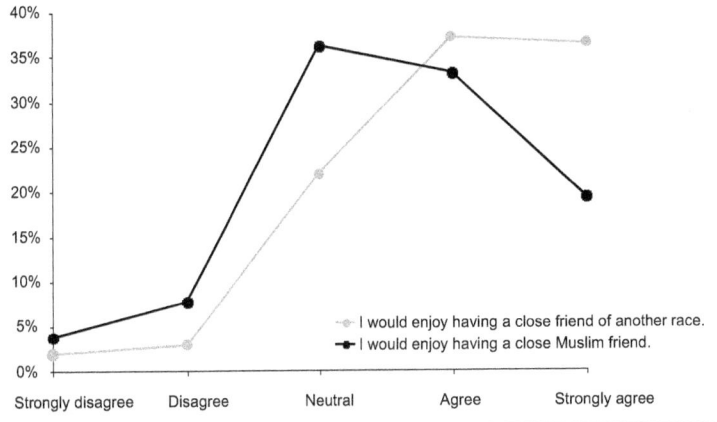

Figure 7.3
Proportion of respondents, by I would enjoy having a close friend of another race/a close Muslim friend.
Note: N = 993 and 997 respectively.

was smallest at the level of 'close friend' with a mean difference of −0.476, $t(984) = -17.4$, $p < .001$ (see Figure 7.3). It was greatest at the level of 'go out with', with a mean difference of −0.894, $t(982) = -26.6$, $p < .001$ (see Figure 7.4), and also at the level of marriage, with a mean difference of −0.894, $t(981) = -25.2$, $p < .001$ (see Figure 7.5). At that level of proximity about 20% of respondents strongly agreed with the statement I would marry someone of

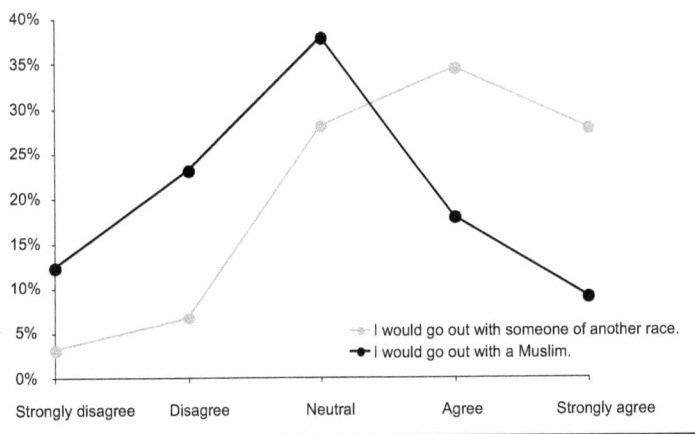

Figure 7.4
Proportion of respondents, by I would go out with someone of another race/a Muslim.
Note: N = 993 and 997 respectively.

another race, but only 7% did so when that 'someone' was a Muslim. This shows that respondents were more reluctant to engage socially with Muslims than those of 'another race'; furthermore, it cannot be explained by a generalised racism but is specific to Muslims.

In order to highlight the differences between social distance towards Muslims as compared persons of 'another race', the difference in responses were ranked (see Figure 7.6). Respondents favoured persons of 'another race' over Muslims on all three measures of social distance, but much more so when the degree of intimacy was greater.

Own versus parents' social distance

Respondents were asked to estimate their parents' social distance as well as their own. When both sets of responses were compared, the differences were either insignificant or, if significant, small. In respect of social distance from a person of 'another race', the mean difference at the level of 'close friend' was -0.01, $t(989) = -0.4$, $p = NS$, at the level of 'go out with' it was -0.08, $t(989) = -2.6$, $p < .01$, and at the level of 'marry' it was 0.03, $t(989) = 1.0$, $p = NS$. In respect of social distance from Muslims, the mean difference at the level of 'close friend' was 0.05, $t(981) = 1.9$, $p = NS$), at the level of 'go out with' it was 0.13, $t(977) = 4.7$, $p < .001$, and at the level of 'marry' it was 0.17, $t(981) = 6.1$, $p < .001$.

These findings show that the social distance of respondents and that of their parents (as perceived by the respondents themselves) were very similar; and where the difference was significant, the parents' social distance was gener-

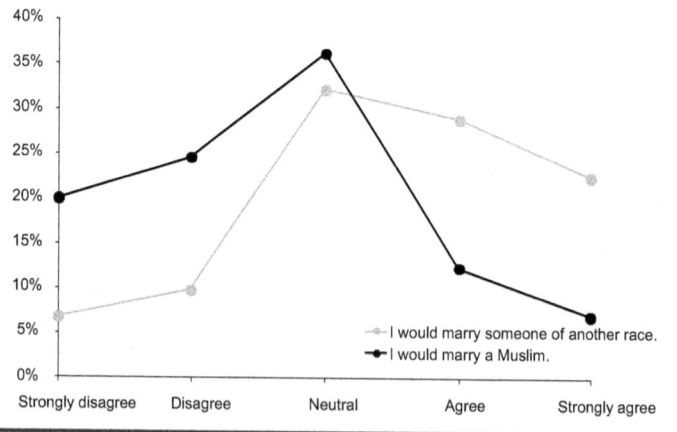

Figure 7.5
Proportion of respondents, by I would marry someone of another race/a Muslim.
Note: *N*= 993 and 997 respectively.

Social Distance From Muslims

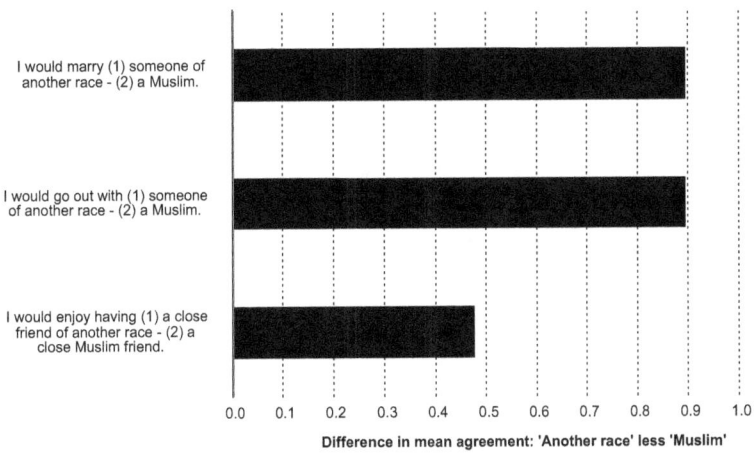

Figure 7.6
Difference in social distance measures: 'Another race' less 'Muslim'.
Note: N= 993 and 997 respectively.

ally slightly greater than that of their children—an unsurprising finding if the older generation is perceived to be socially more conservative than the younger. Because the parent's perceived social distance scores were found to be little different from those of the respondents, they were dropped from the analysis.

How students differ in social distance

These findings show that boys desired not only more social distance in general than did girls, but proportionately more from Muslims than did girls.

As shown in Figure 7.7, a significant difference was found between boys (mean score 7.4) and by girls (6.3) in respect of social distance from 'another race', $F(1,984) = 38.0$, $p < .001$.

A similar pattern was found between boys (mean score 9.6) and by girls (8.6) in respect of social distance from Muslims, $F(1,979) = 26.9$, $p < .001$ (See Figure 7.8).

The role of religion

A significant difference was found between religious affiliations in respect of social distance from 'another race', $F(2,961) = 4.0$, $p < .05$; see Figure 7.9. Post hoc tests (Student-Newman-Keuls, $p < .05$) showed that Catholics (mean score 6.9), desired significantly more social distance from 'another race' than did either Other Christians (6.5) or Non-religious (6.4), but that the latter two groups did not differ significantly one from another.

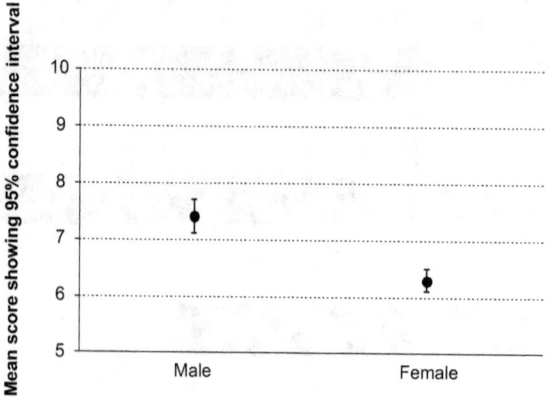

Figure 7.7
Gender differences (another race).

A significant difference was also found between religious affiliations in respect of social distance from Muslims, $F(2,961) = 11.7$, $p < .001$. Post hoc tests (Student-Newman-Keuls, $p < .05$) showed that Catholics (mean score 9.1) and Other Christians (9.4). while not differing significantly one from another, both desired significantly more social distance from Muslims than did Non-religious (8.2; see Figure 7.10).

These findings show that Catholic students desired significantly more social distance from both 'another race' and Muslims than did Non-religious. Other Christians were ambivalent: vis-à-vis 'another race' they resembled Catholics,

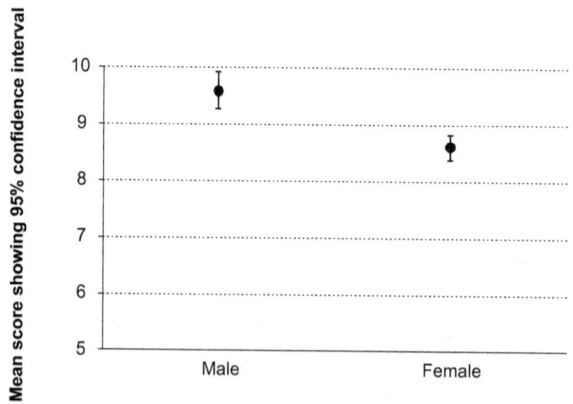

Figure 7.8
Gender differences (Muslims).

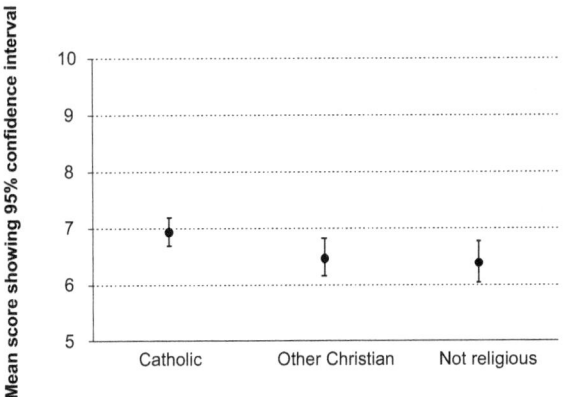

Figure 7.9
Religious differences (another race).

but vis-à-vis Muslims they resembled Non-religious. However, the differences, although significant, were not large.

Does having Muslim friends make a difference?

A significant difference was found between students with Muslim friends (mean score 5.3) and those without (7.1) in respect of social distance from 'another race', $F(1,983) = 72.9$, $p < .001$ (see Figure 7.11).

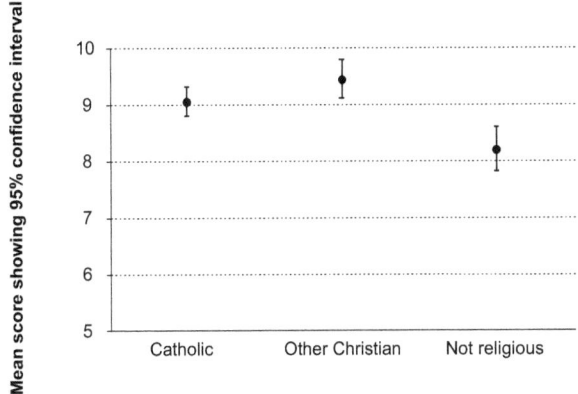

Figure 7.10
Religious differences (Muslims).

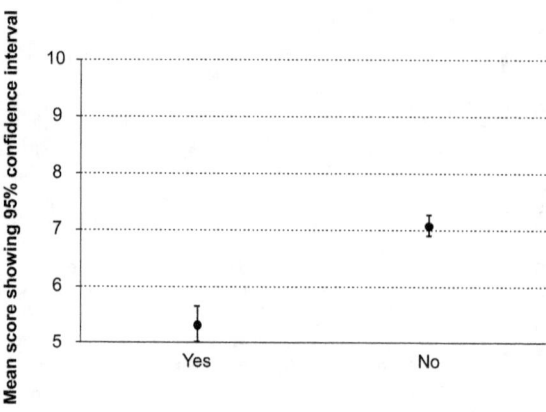

Figure 7.11
Differences (another race).

Also in Figure 7.12, a similar pattern was found between students with Muslim friends (mean score 7.4) and those without (9.4) in respect of social distance from Muslims, $F(1,978) = 83.1$, $p < .001$.

These findings revealed a big difference between students with Muslim friends and those without. At one level this finding is trivial: of course, students with Muslim friends desire less social distance from Muslims. But at another level it raises the question of causality: does having Muslim friends diminish social distance or vice versa? This question cannot be answered by the current study.

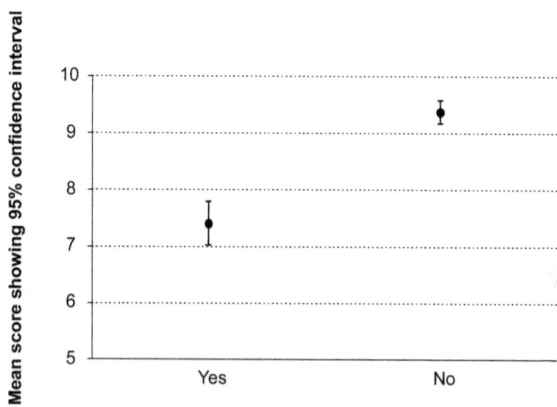

Figure 7.12
Differences (Muslims).

The data revealed another interesting finding: students with Muslim friends not only desire less social distance from Muslims than do those without Muslim friends, they also desire less social distance from 'another race' than do those without Muslim friends. Why? It could be that having Muslim friends opens one up to others different from oneself; or alternatively that whatever causes one to accept Muslims also causes one to accept others. As before, this question goes to causality, and as such cannot be answered by the current study. Evidence of an equally interesting finding emerged with regards to state versus private schools. It shows that students at private schools desired significantly more social distance from Muslims than did those at state schools, but that there was no such distinction in respect of social distance to 'another race'. In other words, all students at both state and private school systems are alike as regards 'another race', but not as regards Muslims.

Recent research points to a strong relationship between the reduction of intergroup prejudice and uncertainty and (a) familiarity and liking and (b) correct social perception of the other. The significance of the first factor shows that alleviating intergroup anxiety leads to a reduction of intergroup feelings of threat (Islam & Hewstone, 1993; Ata, Bastian, Koskinen, & Lusher, 2009). The second demonstrates that distorted perceptions and ambiguous knowledge of the 'other' exaggerate hostile attitudes and endorse hostile behaviour and intention (Lyons & Kashima, 2003).

References

Allport, G.W. (1954). *The nature of prejudice*. Cambridge, MA: Addison-Wesley Pub. Co.

Ata, A. (2007). *Attitudes of school-age non-Muslim Australians to Muslims and Islam: A national survey*. Canberra, Australia: Department of Immigration and Citizenship.

Ata, A., Bastian, B., Koskinen, B., & Lusher, D. (in press). *Intergroup contact in context: Differentiating personal and collective prejudice*.

Hewstone, M. (1990). The 'ultimate attribution error'? A review of the literature on intergroup causal attribution. *European Journal of Social Psychology, 20*, 311–335.

Pettigrew, T.F., & Tropp, L. R. (2006). A Meta-Analytic Test of Intergroup Contact Theory. *Journal of Personality and Social Psychology, 90*(5), 751–783.

Lyons, A., & Kashima, Y. (2003). How are stereotypes maintained through communication? The influence of stereotype sharedness. *Journal of Personality and Social Psychology, 85*(6), 989–1005.

Islam, M., & Hewstone, M. (1993). Intergroup attributions and affective consequences in majority and minority groups. *Journal of Personality and Social Psychology, 64*, 936–950.

Bibliography

Brown, R.J., Condor, S., Mathews, A., Wade, G., & Williams, J.A. (1986). Explaining intergroup differentiation in an industrial organisation. *Journal of Occupational Psychology, 59*, 273–286.

Brown, R., Hinkle, S., Ely, P.G., Fox-Cardamone, L., Maras, P., & Taylor, L.A. (1992). Recognising group diversity: Individualist-collectivist and autonomous-relational social orientations and their implications for intergroup processes. *British Journal of Social Psychology, 31*, 327–342.

Hewstone, M., & Ward, C. (1985). Ethnocentrism and causal attribution in South East Asia. *Journal of Personality and Social Psychology, 48*, 614–623.

Hinkle, S., Brown, R. (1990). Intergroup comparisons and social identity: Some links and lacunae. In D. Abrams & M. A. Hogg (Eds.), *Social identity theory: Constructive and critical advances*. New York, Harvester/Wheatsheaf.

Kelley, H.H., & Michela, J.L. (1980). Attribution theory and research. *Annual Review of Psychology, 31*, 457–503.

Messick, D.M., & Mackie, D. (1989). Intergroup relations. *Annual Review of Social Psychology, 40*, 45-81.

Lusher, D., & Haslam, N. (Eds.) (2007). *Yearning to breathe free: Seeking asylum in Australia*. Sydney, Australia: The Federation Press.

Chapter 8

Attitudes of School-Age Muslim Australians Towards Australia
Gender and Religious Differences: A National Survey

Islam is the third-largest religion in Australia after the Christian denominations and Buddhism, and the Muslim community is one of the fastest growing, having nearly doubled in size between 1996 to 2001. Many are school students, and of these, many are at Islamic schools.

Muslim schools in Australia are newcomers on the national scene, most having been in existence only for the last 15 years. In Victoria alone they employ about 400 teachers, serve 5000 students, and obtain $32 million a year from state and federal governments. Donohoue Clyne (2001) found that although the schools may promote a moral outlook, cultural identity, retention of the mother tongue, and religious practice, many parents expressed concern that these might not be the best alternative to secular education.

The Age (2005, July 31) reported that education departments have little knowledge of the curriculum content in Muslim schools for junior grades, the quality of education on offer, or religious views propagated:

> ... there are concerns among former teachers and members of Melbourne's Islamic community about the overall quality of education the 600-plus students receive .... Muslim extremists were posing a problem for 'vulnerable and impressionable youth' ... [A prominent Muslim leader says that] the proliferation of Islamic schools is causing concern in the Muslim community ... They are accountable to nobody but themselves.

The survey described in this chapter aims to assist policy-makers and curriculum designers to foster intercommunal understanding and cooperation.

In a recent survey titled 'The Great Divide: How Westerners And Muslims View Each Other', the Pew Research Centre (2006) reported that opinions held by the two communities vary markedly by country of origin. Muslims were more positive than the general public in their adopted country about their future, but many worried about the future of Muslims in their country of origin. Their greatest concern was unemployment. Islamic extremism emerged as the number 2 concern. The majority do not regard most non-Muslims as hostile towards Muslims.

Clearly, even on this preliminary comparison, there is much commonality in our respective findings, and much common ground on which to build.

We know from previous work with non-Muslim students that there is goodwill but much ignorance towards Muslims. At the same time, we know little about the opinions of Muslim students. For consistency, policy should be informed by the viewpoints of both groups.

Companion Study of Non-Muslim Students

The current study, commissioned by the Department of Immigration and Citizenship (DIAC) follows a previous study also commissioned by DIAC entitled 'How Australian Students see Islam and Muslims' — hereafter referred to as the companion study (see Chapter 3). The aim of that study was to 'identify, analyse and interpret the knowledge, perception and attitudes of Year 11 students with respect to Islam and the Muslim communities'. The two studies are largely complementary in the sense that both explore how one community perceives the other.

Because the companion study drew its survey sample from non-denominational and Christian denominational schools, it included few if any Muslims; it can therefore fairly be said to represent how the non-Muslim student community views Islam and the Muslim. Conversely, because the current study drew its survey sample from Muslim denominational schools, it included few if any non-Muslims; it can therefore fairly be said to represent how the overwhelmingly Muslim student community views mainstream Australian society.

It should be noted that the survey samples of the two studies differ not according to the religion (or non-religion) of the students but according to the denomination (or non-denomination) of the schools they attend. This was done both for sampling convenience (it would have been difficult to sample in any other way) and because we felt it would have been invidious to select students on religious grounds within a school setting. Nevertheless, since nearly all students at non-Muslim schools are themselves not Muslims, and since those at Muslim schools are nearly all Muslim, in practice one can interpret the surveys as reciprocal viewpoints.

Survey Method and Sample Characteristics

The survey unit was the high-school student. Over 430 completed questionnaires were obtained from students at eight schools (six high schools and two community schools) in Victoria, New South Wales, Queensland and Western Australia. South Australia, the Northern Territory, Australian Capital Territory, and Tasmania did not take part for logistical reasons. Two schools catered mainly for students of Turkish background.

Schools were requested to survey Year 11 students, these being considered mature enough to give informed answers. The survey was administered to eligible students present on the day of the survey. Even so, four of the schools chose to administer the survey to Years 10 and 12.

As the survey was administered under the auspices of each school, and in class, it is unlikely that there was any significant nonresponse at the student level. However, certain schools and school agencies declined to participate.

Many school principals and school agencies were supportive. They suggested that the survey was in the best interest of all Australians. However, most of them declined to consider participating in the survey prior to meeting with the chief researcher and assessing his credentials. One of the community principals, an imam, insisted that the researcher meet with him at his home.

Only one principal of European background sent his approval to conduct the survey promptly by email. He indicated that the survey was relevant to Year 11 students of Religious Education, and that they should be encouraged to explore the beliefs of other religions whenever that was possible.

The survey was refined in the light of the pilot, after which 431 students were administered the full survey form. The percentage of female participant students (57%) was slightly higher than male students (43%). Almost the entire sample (93%) declared themselves to be Muslim. We do not know the circumstances of those who gave 'Other' (i.e., not Muslim) as their religion. It is possible that some were children of interreligious marriages, and others just rebellious. There were more students born in Australia (61%) than overseas (39%). However, the percentage of fathers (3%) and mothers (9%) born in Australia was significantly lower.

Over 66% indicated that their friends were mostly Muslim and 3% indicated that they were mostly non-Muslim; the remainder were 'half and half'.

Most students (93%) spoke other languages at home. This accords with the finding that most parents were born overseas. In the companion study only 19% non-Muslim Australian students spoke other languages at home.

Respondents were presented with 18 statements concerning subjective attitudes towards Islam and Muslims and asked to rate their agreement on a three-point scale of *Agree* through *Neutral* to *Disagree*.

Findings

Between a third and a half of the sample was neutral for many questions, indicating that they neither agreed nor disagreed with the statement (see Figure 8.1). This could signify honest ignorance of the issues or alternatively lack of motivation.

This contrasts with the companion study, which found that a considerably higher proportion of neutral responses given by non-Muslim students to comparable (and in some cases identical) questions concerning Islam and Muslims. This suggests that Muslim students are either more informed about, or more motivated to comment on the position of Muslims in Australia than are non-Muslims — understandably so, as they are commenting on their own community, not someone else's.

Figure 8.1 reveals the attitudes of the sample as a whole. But does this mask differences within the sample? For instance, do boys differ systematically from girls in their attitudes towards Islam and Muslims? To answer this and similar questions, we used statistical techniques to determine if there were significant differences in the mean attitudes of all the demographic groups measured in the survey.

Gender differences

Boys and girls differed significantly on three out of 18 statements (see Figure 8.2). This contrasts with the companion study, which found that non-Muslim students boys and girls differed significantly on 16 out of 23 questions.

Boys agreed significantly more than girls with the proposition 'Most non-Muslim Australians want good relations with the Muslim community'; and disagreed less with 'The image of Muslims is as good as other migrant groups in Australia'. Unlike girls, who disagreed, boys were neutral on the proposition 'Islamic values clash with Australian values'.

The role of religion

Students who stated their religion as Muslim differed significantly from those who stated 'Other religion' on seven out of 18 statements (Figure 8.3). The 'Other' group appear to on the whole unsympathetic and critical of Muslims. For example, they thought Muslims were portrayed fairly in the media; the Muslim group did not. And they disagreed with proposition 'Most Muslim Australians want good relations with the non-Muslim community'.

Attitudes of School-Age Muslim Australians Towards Australia

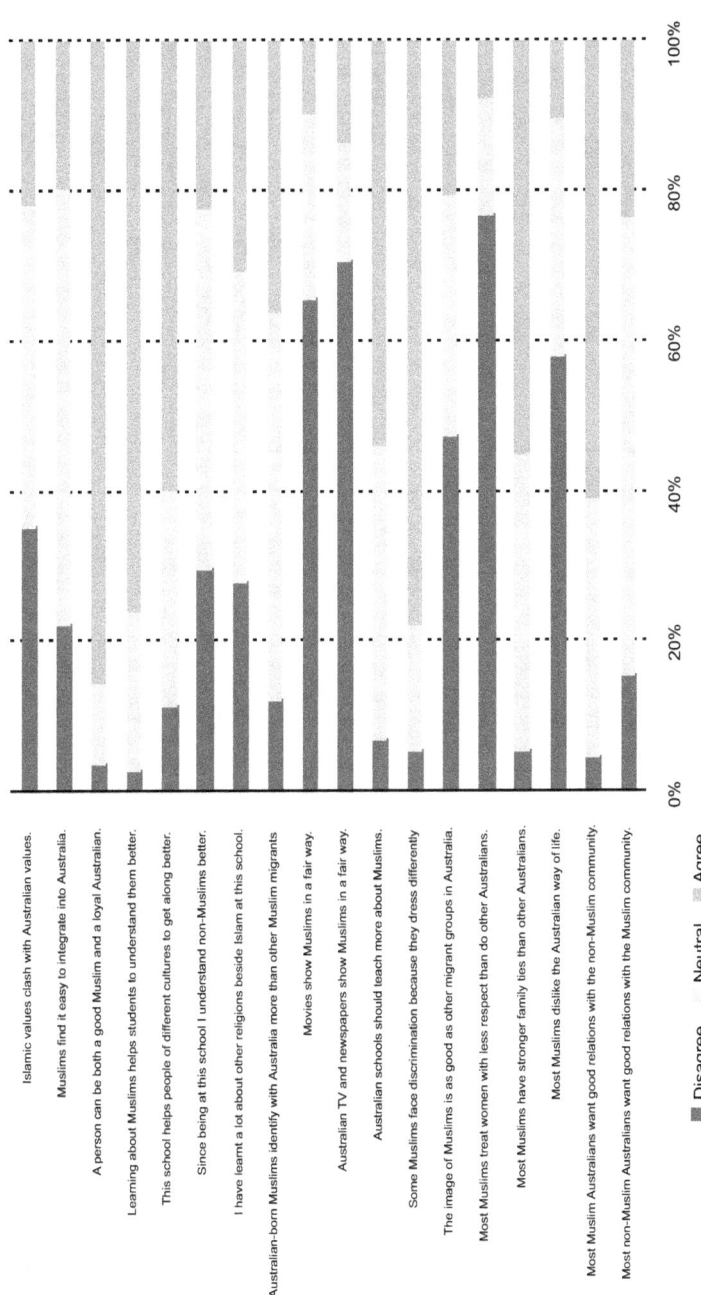

Figure 8.1
Proportion of responses.

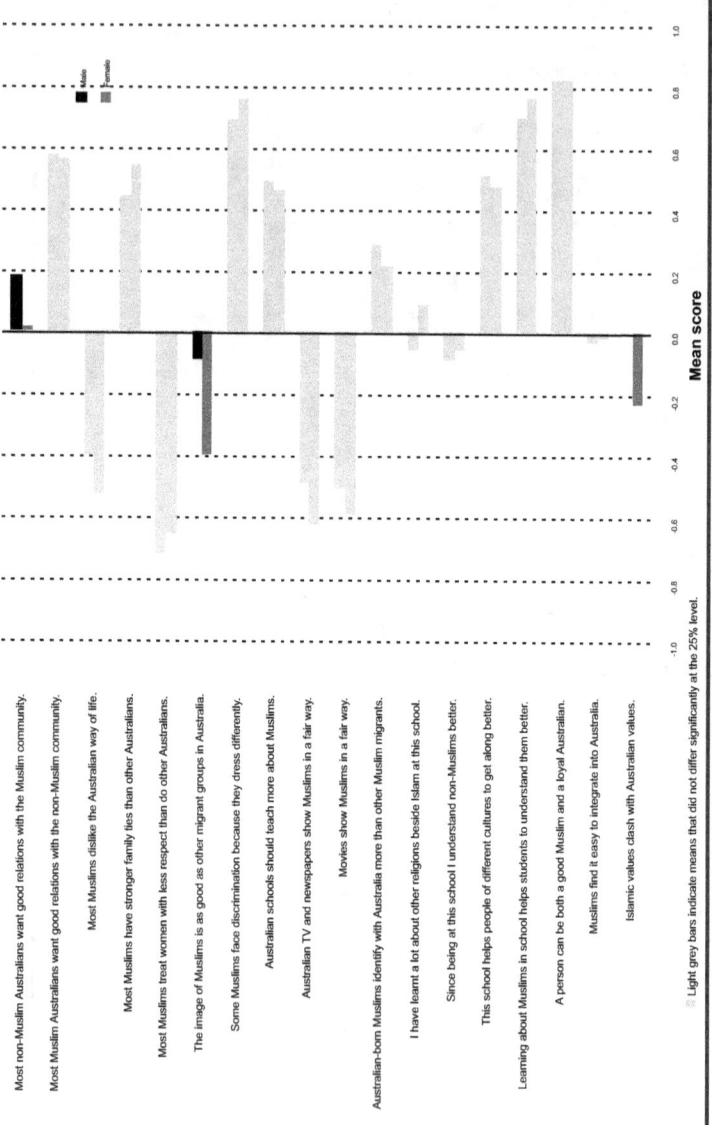

Figure 8.2
Mean attitude scores, by sex.

Although significant in a statistical sense, it should be noted that the differences are based on a very small sample of students claiming 'Other' religion (11 persons). The findings must therefore be interpreted with caution. Moreover, they come from respondents in quite unusual circumstances: a religious (or non-religious) minority at overtly religious schools. It might be that all their responses, including their claim to a religion other than Islam, are motivated by another factor altogether — a pervading rebelliousness to authority, perhaps.

Respondents were presented with 18 statements concerning subjective attitudes towards Islam and Muslims and asked to rate their agreement on a three-point scale of 'Agree' through 'Neutral' to 'Disagree'.

Does the religion of one's friends make a difference?

Those with mostly Muslim friends differed significantly from those with mostly non-Muslim friends (although not significantly from those with a balance from both communities) on four out of 18 statements (Figure 8.3).

Not surprisingly, those with mostly Muslim friends held more empathetic attitudes towards Muslims than did those with mostly non-Muslim friends (although we are naturally not in a position distinguish cause and effect on this evidence alone). Most noticeable is the divergence of views on how Muslims are portrayed by the media: those with mostly non-Muslim friends say fairly; those with mostly Muslim friends demur.

Selected responses to 'What are the first words that come to your mind when you hear the word 'Australian'
People that try to make a better community and people who just laze around with a VB can in their hand.
I seriously think of alcohol … but I also think of hard-working people and kind people.
Homeland, Australian flag?
People with beers in their hand watching footy.
Dirty people and drinking and drugs.
Fear, because I have the fear of being abused for being a Muslim.
Australians are European people who think of Jesus to be son of God which is impossible, and are fairly good people.

Selected responses to What are the first words that come to your mind when you hear the word 'Muslim'
I know it is wrong to say, but terrorist.
In newspaper articles, there has been signs of saying No to them.

Us & Them: Muslim–Christian Relations and Cultural Harmony in Australia

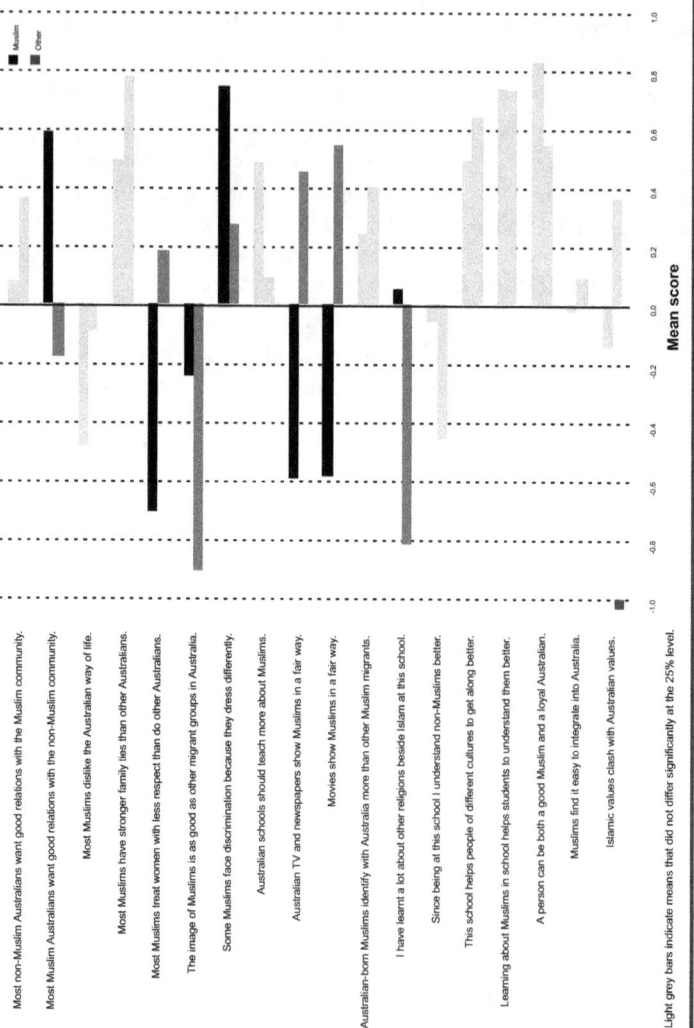

Figure 8.3
Mean attitude scores, by religion.

118

Open-ended questions concerning Muslims

Two open-ended questions were put to respondents and the answers coded into a manageable number of categories as shown below. Naturally this entailed a degree of subjective judgment.

What are the first words that come to your mind when you hear the word 'Muslim'?

When asked for the first words that come to mind when the word 'Muslim' is mentioned, roughly a third of the respondents (35%) offered comments that were faith-related, including 'religious', 'pious to Allah', 'Prophet Muhammad' and 'Islam'. Another 31% offered positive comments, including 'being trustworthy', 'reliable', 'defending their religion without any fear', and 'being true to their tradition and community'. Words indicating 'terrorism', 'terrorising' and 'terrorist' comprised 11% of the response; and these in combination with another positive comment including 'being dedicated to their cause' registered 3% of the responses. Only 6% mentioned discrimination, and 3% gave comments of little or no relevance including 'apathy of the media and everyone'; 8% gave no response. See Figure 8.4.

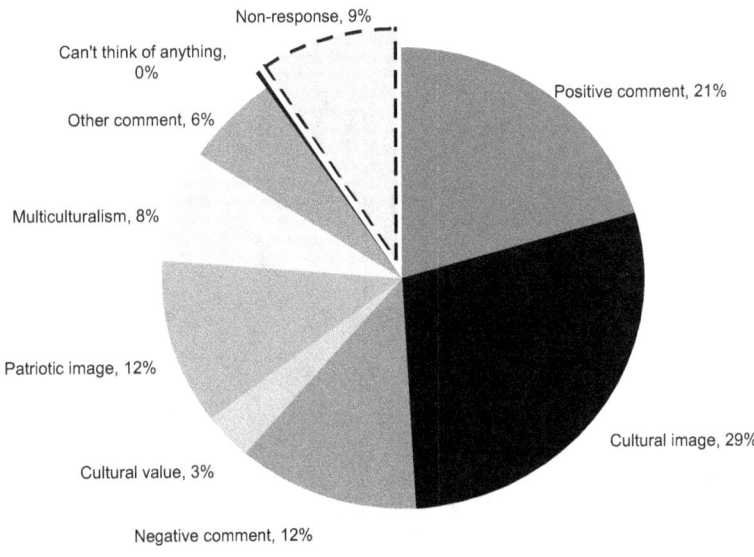

Figure 8.4
Response to 'What are the first words that come to your mind when you hear the word "Australian"'.
Note: 431 participants (inc. non-response).

What are the first words that come to your mind when you hear the word 'Australian'?

When asked for the first words that come [to] mind when the word 'Australian' is mentioned, just under one-third (29%) offered neutral or negative comments, specifically relating to cultural images or symbols, including the words 'Cronulla', 'bogan', 'boogan', 'beer', 'drugs', 'the bush', 'Howard', 'Christian', 'blonds', 'fags', 'pussies', 'gay', 'cricket', 'freckles', 'BBQ' and 'thongs'. About 21% offered positive qualities, including 'peaceful', 'cultured', 'nice', 'easygoing', 'OK people' and 'freedom'. A smaller group (8%) referred to multiculturalism; 12% referred to patriotic qualities, including 'Australia my country', 'I am born in Australia'; 3% referred to culture-based values, including 'a fair go' and 'mateship'. One in ten (2%) offered generalised negative comments, including 'being lost', 'confused', 'dickheads', 'rednecks', 'hostile', 'arrogant', 'greedy', 'non-believers' and 'racist'. About one respondent in eleven (9%) offered no response. See Figure 8.5.

Conclusions

This survey and the companion study show that many students have little or no knowledge about the historical roots of clash, contradictions and dialogue between faiths, or about avenues towards cooperation and integration between

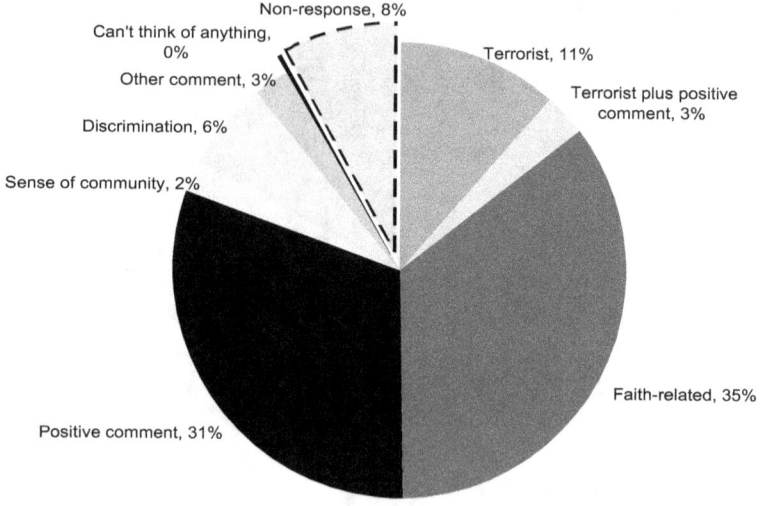

Figure 8.5
Response to 'What are the first words that come to your mind when you hear the word "Muslim"'.
Note: 431 participants (inc. non-response).

members of the various religious communities. Are there casual links between knowledge of, and attitudes towards Christianity and mainstream Australia and if so, which way does it rub? The survey found considerable lack of knowledge of Christianity; almost half of the students recorded a *Don't know* response to all questions; and, for example, only 17% correctly disagreed with the statement 'Jesus wrote the Bible'. Indeed, a significant percentage of students from the two DIAC-funded national surveys in Muslim and non-Muslim schools believed that their image of 'the other' was greatly influenced by what they read and hear in the media. Content analysis of a random sample of both the Muslim and Australia press revealed the extent and influence of stereotyping on the perception of students.

There are clearly grounds for this belief. Because in most Islamic countries the mass media is controlled, the question of why Australian television does not help change the negative image and dispense with some honest remains a moot one. The perception that local television is market oriented and is not a free medium to educate the public but is dedicated to the perpetuation of social structure remains strong.

When asked what they liked most about non-Muslim Australians, nearly half (46%) offered positive comments (compared with 31% regarding Muslim Australians). These include phrases such as 'solidarity and uniqueness', 'smile back', 'relaxed life', 'caring', 'even-handed', 'not judgmental', 'enjoy life', 'don't act mean', 'down to earth' and 'kind'. (Noteworthy that none of these comments were offered to Muslim Australians, possibly because of difference in the hierarchy of values.) Some 17% gave mixed comments including: 'Some are nice but others judge Muslims Australians by what they see in the media'; 'Some are friendly — they know how to have fun without getting into trouble'. Another 5% offered 'other comments' including 'look nice', 'sheilas', 'their accent', 'world soccer', 'care for nature', 'their food', and 'dressing well'.

When asked about what they like least about Muslim–Australians roughly 2 out of 5 (42%) gave a no response (31%) or could not think of anything (11%). Some 10% alluded to antagonism' offering comments including 'they live on the government', 'they don't mix', 'don't give Aussies a chance', 'give Australia a bad name', 'don't blend', and 'feel superior'. Another 11% offered negative comments, including 'violent', 'narrow-minded', 'quarrelsome', 'give a bad image', 'make mistakes', 'don't obey the law', 'greedy', 'arrogant in public', 'opportunistic', and 'their attitude'. In contrast 13% gave 'qualified' negative comments including 'some are sexist', 'many are not modest', 'a few are religious', 'a few are lazy'. The response relating to 'defensive' drew 3%, and 'neglecting their religion', 12%.

Clearly much work is needed to remedy these attitudes. Providing awareness sessions to students and parents that address critical social, religious and cultural issues could include topics like 'stereotyping and inclusivity', 'freedom of expression and the media', 'sexual permissiveness and conservativeness', 'secular and religious identity', 'individual and community basic rights', and 'social justice and foreign policy'.

Another measure could explore how Muslim schools promote intercultural understanding. The survey found that students were equally divided on statements that their school teaches them.

Exploring the casual link between social distance from, and attitudes towards, Islam and Muslims is another step to take. It was found that at the level of 'close friend' the non-Muslims were more accepting of non-Muslims than were the non-Muslims of Muslims; but at the level of 'marry' the situation was reversed. This is a significant discovery and warrants further investigation.

Acknowledgment

The research presented in this chapter was funded by the Department of Immigration and Citizenship.

Reference

Donohoue Clyne, I. (2001). Educating Muslim children in Australia. In A. Saeed & S. Akbarzadeh (Eds.), *Muslim communities in Australia* (pp. 116–137). Sydney, Australia: UNSW Press.

Pew Research Centre. (2006). *The great divide: How Westerners and Muslims view each other.* Available at http://pewglobal.org/reports/display.php?ReportID=253

Bibliography

Asmar, C. (2001). A community on campus: Muslim students in Australian universities. In S. Akbarzadeh & A. Saeed (Eds.), *Muslim communities in Australia.* Sydney: UNSW Press.

Ata, A. (2007). *How Australian students see Islam and Muslims: A national survey* (unpublished). Department of Immigration and Citizenship.

Ata, A. (2006). Demonising Australia's Christian and Muslim Arabs in Cartoons. *Compass, 40,* 31–34.

Ata, A. (2006) Observing different faiths, learning about ourselves: Practice with intermarried Muslims and Christians. *Australian Social Work, 59*(3), 250–264.

Ata, A. (2006) Lost in translation: Australia's top cleric. *Australian e-Journal of Social Debate.*

Ata, A., & Furlong, M. (2005). Observing different faiths, learning about ourselves: Practice with inter-married Muslims and Christians. *Australian and New Zealand Journal of Family Therapy, 26*(4), 200–209.

Ata, A. (2005) Dynamics of the interfaith marriage: The Australian Christians and Muslims. *Eastern Anthropologist, 50,* 187–199.

Ata, A. (2005). Cross religious misunderstanding or a clash between civilizations in Australia *Current Dialogue, 44.*

Ata, A., & Batrouney, T. (1989). Attitudes and stereotyping in Victorian secondary schools. *The Eastern Anthropologist, 42*(1).

Australian Arabic Council. (2001). *Increase in racial vilification in light of terror attacks: September 2001* (Australian Arabic Council Report). Melbourne, Australia: Author.

Brasted, H. (2001). Contested representations in historical perspective: Images of Islam and the Australian press 1950-2000. In S. Akbarzadeh & A. Saeed (Eds.), *Muslim communities in Australia*. Sydney, Australia: UNSW Press.

Bullivant, B.M. (1987). *The ethnic encounter in the secondary school: Ethno-cultural reproduction and resistance: Theory and case studies*. London; New York: Falmer Press.

Bullivant, B.M. (1988). The ethnic success ethic challenges conventional wisdom about immigrant disadvantages in Australia. *Australian Journal of Education, 32*(2), 223–243.

Cahill, D., & Gundert, A. (1996). *Immigration and schooling in the 1990s*. Canberra, Australia: Bureau of Immigration Multicultural and Population Research and Department of Immigration and Multicultural Affairs.

Donohoue Clyne, I. (2000). *Seeking education: The struggle of Muslims to educate their children in Australia.* Unpublished PhD thesis, University of Melbourne, Australia.

Dunn, K. (2001). The geography of racisms in NSW: A theoretical exploration and some preliminary findings from the mid-1990s. *The Australian Geographer, 32*(1), 29–44.

Dunn, K. (2004). Islam in Australia: Contesting the discourse of absence. *The Australian Geographer, 53*(3), 333–353.

Dunn, K. (2005). Australian public knowledge of Islam. Studia Islamika. *Indonesian Journal for Islamic Studies, 12*(1), 1–32.

Kalantzis, M., & Cope, B. (1984). Multiculturalism and education policy. In G. Bottomley & M.M. De Lepervanche (Eds.), *Ethnicity, class and gender in Australia*. Sydney, Australia: George Allen & Unwin.

Muslim Community Reference Group. (2006). *Building on social cohesion, harmony and security.* Canberra, Australia: Author.

Poynting, S. (2002). 'Bin Laden in the suburbs': Attacks on Arab and Muslim Australians before and after 11 September. *Current Issues in Criminal Justice, 14*(1), 43–64.

Rieder, J. (1985). *Canarsie: The Jews and Italians of Brooklyn against liberalism*. Cambridge, MA: Harvard University Press.

Said, E. (1981). *Covering Islam: How the media and the experts determine how we see the rest of the world.* New York: Pantheon Books.

Said, E. (1995). *Orientalism*. New York: Penguin.

Simkin, K., & Gauci, E. (1992). Ethnic diversity and multicultural education. In R.J. Burns & A.R. Welch (Eds.), *Contemporary perspectives in comparative education*. New York: Garland.

Speck, B.W. (1997). Respect for religious differences: The case of Muslim students. *New Directions for Teaching and Learning, 70,* 39–46.

Windle, J. (2004). Schooling, symbolism and social power: The Hijab in republican France. *Australian Educational Researcher, 31*(1), 95–112.

Section Three

Muslim–Christian Intermarriage

Chapter 9

Adjustment and Complications
of Christian–Muslim Intermarriages in Australia

It has been said that marriage is the triumph of imagination over intelligence. Who we marry, and why, are questions that have occupied the minds and hearts of people for centuries. People can marry those who are similar to themselves, or those who are different. Intermarriage implies the crossing of ethnic, linguistic, religious, racial or national boundaries by a woman and a man in life's most intimate union. We exclude arranged, mail-order or 'shotgun' marriages because of the element of coercion.

Intermarriage is arguably the best indicator as to whether a particular group is fully integrated into and accepted by the mainstream community. Marriage, being the most committed and intimate of relationships can indicate that there is no prejudice between members of the host and minority communities. This suggests that interfaith dialogue and tolerance are an integral part of the two communities, as reflected within interfaith families. It may also mean that guardians of the ethnic or minority traditions have lost hold on their members, and, in particular, those from the first generation in relation to members of the second generation (Birrell & Healy, 2000).

The increasing occurrence of intermarriages across international barriers is an aspect of globalisation frequently overlooked. Intercultural couples strolling arm-in-arm are increasingly seen as one consequence of the movements of peoples across the world, whether as tourists or professionals, contract workers or permanent migrants. Findings continue to show that intermarried couples are more likely to be above average in educational level, to both be working, and are less likely to be unemployed.

In the case of Australia there has not been much systematic study of intermarriage between Muslims and Christians. Studying such intermarriage can help us look at the merging of the two communities at personal and social levels, and their identity, religious conversion, dress code, upbringing of children and national aspiration. Such a study can shed light on the evolution of the Australian family while the community is in a process of transition.

Intermarriage is of particular interest because it is one of the last stages towards full integration of one group with another (Price, 1994). It can be viewed as an index of the full acceptance of both partners into the wider society (Blau, Blum, & Schwartz, 1982).

Some researchers have produced evidence that such intermarriages will preserve and strengthen the boundaries of the individual's identity; others have argued that they will ultimately weaken and erode them (Quadagno, 1981).

Other studies have shown that it is possible to embody multiple identities, and that parts of one's customs can be preserved. Price (1993) studied intermarriage rates for the second generation of interethnic marriages and found that they were higher than the first generation by 10 to 60%, depending on the type of ethnic community.

In the early days of a relationship, as couples move closer to knowing one another, misunderstandings are not normally of a serious nature. Once they are more comfortable with each other they may have to work harder to deal with perceived difficulties and other conflicts. People are inclined to find a resolution within their interfaith status, readjusting earlier relationships with members of their own community, especially those who do not take kindly to mixed marriages.

Students of comparative cultural and ethnic studies are keen to show that in traditional non-Western societies, intermarried couples who appear and act as a solid unit, despite residual inner feelings of tension, have been a fact of life. The unexpected problems associated with family members living different lifestyles results primarily from the psychosocial allegiances to one's psychoreligious upbringing, which has been nurtured alongside members of one's previous extended family (Ata, 2000).

The nature of the composition of migrant families, and the dispersal of ethno-religious communities across Australian cities softens the obligations that intermarried couples feel from their religious communities. For women, Christian or Muslim, the effect of coming to a new home is closely entwined with adjusting to a new lifestyle with a different religious and cultural aura. Adjustment means a psychological and behavioural adaptation — a coming into another established system without being able to predict the consequences. It does not mean adoption of new religious practices and behaviour, even though the leaders of Muslim communities normally require the partner to publicly declare their conversion to Islam at the time of marriage. This observation applies to a large number of interviewees in the study described in this chapter.

Behind the various perceptions of the status of their interfaith marriages there lies a range of common techniques to resolve the differences in marriage. As these kinds of marriages become accepted, newer approaches and resolution mechanisms develop.

The reactions collected in this study are placed under the following six patterns:

1. Conversion or annexation

This is when one spouse converts to the life and faith of the other. Estimates in this survey show that this option is stated (although not necessarily chosen at will) by 19%. In order to rule out any friction due to religious differences, such a conversion has to be free of pressure, sincere, and the person's own choice.

However, the spouses who have given up their religion and faith may face ongoing problems. They may find it difficult to replace familiar ways of thinking and feeling with new ones. In time they may feel resentment toward their partner, however fully the conversion ritual may have been explained to them beforehand.

One participant who felt angry commented, 'You can't marry a chicken and a rooster. It is not on'.

Missing the practices associated with their religious tradition was expressed by another participant: 'We seem to go to whatever function his community puts on. The children sense that it is one-way traffic, but for how long?'.

2. A policy of ignoring and withdrawal

In this case, both partners withdraw from organised religious activities. They cease to be open to religious discussions and avoid them within their household. Choosing a policy of ignoring as a way of dealing with difference may lead to unexpected surprises when there is a family crisis. In the long term, this decision is not regarded as successful. Later in life and particularly after the birth of children, one of the partners, with an activated nostalgia, may try to become more active in their faith again — possibly in an attempt to tie their children to their original faith. In doing so, they discover it is hard to suppress their spirituality, and to ignore their differences.

3. A strategy of diversity and plurality in faith

In this situation both partners have several choices. Together they might decide to go to one partner's religious service one week and to the alternative one the next week. With the support from one another and from their respective institutions, they might even join each other's churches.

Through understanding, they honour the uniqueness and wholesomeness of each faith, choosing not to 'homogenise' religious differences. Not only does their lifestyle create an opportunity to honour both traditions, but they have also paved the way for their children to thrive within an enriched context. One interviewee's response to this choice was, 'It is a case of creating healthy boundaries; a sort of religious pluralism that allows considerable overlap in world views; in ensuring peaceful coexistence and complimenting the life of one another'.

4. Compromising and negotiating

In this situation both partners choose to leave their affiliated religion and move into one where they will meet each other halfway. For some it is an open-ended story. For others it replicates an unfinished symphony — a case where partners make certain promises and eventually backpedal so as to keep the upper hand if circumstances do not favour them. In such a situation, one has to ask if marriage is to be only a power struggle why marry at all?

It is estimated that 30% of intrafaith couples select this option — for example, a Catholic/Greek Orthodox couple switch over to the Anglican or Uniting Church. No accurate figures have been secured to determine the percentages of interfaith couples (e.g., Muslim/Christian, or Jewish/Muslim) who make this kind of conversion.

In the light of this situation, social scientists have developed a 'Belief System Selector' kit, a test designed to help couples locate a faith that matches their already existing religious and spiritual beliefs. By finding a faith they both rate highly, the spouses can be assured of fitting in with their select faith group.

Taking the opposite direction from compromise, both couples may select to sever their affiliation with their respective faiths. Whether this guarantees a resolution of religious and cultural differences, which operate on a subconscious level, one can not be certain. Severing ties with one's religion is common among those who feel that their commitment is at a low ebb anyway, and who feel that religion plays a small part in their life.

5. Pastoral–ecumenical yielding

The couples endeavour to integrate both their faith traditions and spiritual guidelines into their family life. They may do so in creative ways that forge a common ground, uniting family members. This merger may not satisfy conservative communities, who tend to view such a process as involving dangerous compromises.

6. Versatile outlook–worldview

Couples may choose to remain respectful and non-judgemental towards each other's religious tradition. Their willingness to give one another freedom to practise their religion helps set ground rules to make communication pleasant and safe. Respecting the other's 'otherness' and not being inclined to make the other like oneself, may reduce all differences to a lowest common denominator. Such unity within diversity, however, adds more richness and beauty to marital life, these people argue, particularly when raising children.

While celebrating religious practices and holy days separately may enrich family environment, it can also trigger crises, because it may reduce the amount of time that families spend together and reduce the level of companionship in their marriage. Complaints of this sort were voiced by many couples.

One sceptical woman said (Interview 47; Ata, 1980):

> I keep wondering why our kids find it more confusing to make sense out of going to one church one week and another place of worship recommended by their father. How can we make a decision on whether to baptise them in which church, both of them or none at all, without feeling any regret! And where will we educate them — in a secular or religious school? Maybe it is good that the kids are still young and as long as we identify potential problems and state our position honestly things will be OK. We won't dismiss our faith; we agreed from day one to accommodate each other's feelings. And so we will put each other's feelings before the dictates of our religious beliefs.

Methodology

A sample size of 106 people formed the basis of analysis. They were selected from Victoria, with the majority being residents of Melbourne. The number, although considered small for a comprehensive study, has formed an exhaustive study over a period of several months. There were 44 Muslim and 19 Christian male participants; and 33 Muslim and 10 Christian female participants of which only 28% were born in Australia. The remainder were born in Europe (48%), in Asia (15%) and in the Middle East (Table 9.1).

A sizable group (48%) indicated that they have fully or partly completed their tertiary education.

Other demographic data reveal that 85% have obtained Australian citizenship; the remainder are either migrants or decided not to initiate a

Table 9.1
Sex and Religion of Participants (Before Marriages)

Males		Females	
Muslim	44	Muslim	33
Christian	19	Christian	10
Total	63	Total	43

requested for naturalisation. Of the former group 72% were born in Australia compared with 58% of their partners. The remainder cited Europe (mainly East Europe), non-Muslim Asia, the Middle East and other Muslim countries, including Pakistan and Malaysia. Of the total participants 43% were able to speak English as their first language (Table 9.2).

The shift of Christian partners affiliating with their Muslim spouse is clearly evident. When the gender breakdown factor is introduced, one notices a greater shift among Christian female spouses toward the Muslim faith. Identifying with either religion after marriage, even though half of the participants reported choosing civil marriages, is a factor that will be clarified elsewhere.

Adjustment

For women, whether Christian or Muslim, the effect of coming to a new home is closely intertwined with adjusting to a new lifestyle with a different religious and cultural environment. Adjustment here means a psychological and behavioural adaptation, without being able to predict the consequences. It does not necessarily mean adoption of religious practices and behaviours, even though the leaders of the community to which the Muslim spouse belongs normally require the partner to declare publicly their conversion to Islam at the time of marriage. This may not mean a total assimilation into the mainstream group, but is generally accepted as a sign of compliance. The spouse may not be pressured to interact with members of the other group, nor to adopt an active role.

Mixed marriages have at times evoked extreme reactions from groups that suddenly found themselves connected. Dormant emotions, ranging from fear of the unknown, impregnation of cultural purity, destabilisation of the community's identity, to outright xenophobia, find their way to the surface. Perhaps the most difficult problem for couples is the changing role they face as a result of expectations from their community and partners.

Changed patterns of living are unavoidable as these are forced on or assumed by one of the spouses. Like monocultural and same religious marriages, the relationship or power base between the spouses is never equal. In making decisions, domestic or financial, the family goes through a number

Table 9.2
Religion Before and After Marriage

Religion	Self		Partner	
	Before	After	Before	After
Muslim	73%	81%	26%	35%
Christian	27%	19%	74%	65%

of difficult stages. How willing and adaptable each spouse is towards the other will decide the success of their acknowledgment of the differences.

In addition, same-religion couples have to make additional adjustments to other cultural demands. The potential for greater problems becomes real if one spouse was brought up in a modern culture and the other in a traditional one. An example may be when the wife is expected to perform a traditional role at home but decides to establish a place for herself outside the domestic environment.

Often these roles are contradictory to the norms of their country of origin. For example, the assumed right of the parents to resort to physical admonishment of their children, or the husband of his wife, is replaced with actionable litigation. The unquestioned right of the older son to inherit his parents' house upon the death of his father is a premigration practice that is not recognised in a society like Australia. Likewise, the wife's entitlement to half of the residence 2 years after marriage is considered unthinkable in traditional societies.

For centuries, Muslim theological leadership has introduced laws and regulations for interreligious marriages. As guardians of social cohesion these leaders had a clear mandate to protect people against extramarital strains and the anxiety of overcoming cultural obstacles.

Prescriptions for successful marriages have been laid out in substance and detail. The Sharia, or the Divine Law, is a mixture of ethics, ritual and good manners — theological thought grafted onto canon law.

Early Muslim scholars, like Al-Ghazali, make virginity for the bride a precondition for a successful marriage. They argue that not only does it engender love and stability, but any suitor would be repulsed to know that his wife has been touched by another man. Says Al-Ghazali, 'the surest love is that which is engendered with the first loved one' (n.d.).

Other qualities that must be sought in the bride are good character, piety, beauty, a dowry, ability to bear children, lineage, and not being a close relative.

Spirituality has been the preferred quality for women as advocated by the Prophet. He said: 'Men marry women for four things, namely, wealth, status and family, beauty and righteousness; but you should prefer righteousness [as the reason for selecting a spouse]' (Bajeva, p. 51).

This specific point conjures up a possibility that the religious polarisation may itself raise additional anxieties and crises. It may also be precipitated by personality types of the spouses, and may thus lead to an exaggeration of differences.

Differences between male and female participants widen in regard to permitting their children the choice of their own religion. Of the university educated, almost 51% give permission to choose, compared with 40% of those with secondary school education. Almost 28% of the latter group gave a 'no response' compared with 17% in the former.

It has been suggested that women may marry men of a different religion to avoid sexist and other patriarchal attitudes. For example, Greek women in Australia avoid marrying Greek males, as they are seen to embody narrow and old-fashioned notions of gender roles. Out-marriages between Greek women and non-Greek men are more likely to survive than in-marriages.

Data predicting the survival of Australian interreligious marriages compared to single religious marriages is not readily available. In time, sufficient numbers of intermarried couples will make such an analysis possible.

Negative features of Muslim–Christian marriages

Restrictions relating to gender roles range from those imposed by the religious community, to those that are self-imposed so as to avoid disharmonies with a curious neighbourhood. While there may be commonality in food, modes of discipline, and national celebrations between the couples, new nuances of communication, expectations and adjustment take shape. Many statements to this effect arose during the interviews. Subtle differences in the lifestyles between the two religious communities were highlighted. Couples cited differences between modern versus traditional backgrounds, cultural expectations entwined with gender roles, and the shifting of attention from the husband to the children. The elements of restricted or liberal behaviour, an adventurous or family-oriented outlook and freedom of expression are deeply embedded in the two communities.

A high proportion of spouses experienced upheavals in their lives before they became married, in addition to the usual premigration-related hardships. This may have triggered the need for them to pursue change in their lives. It may also be why they were drawn to their counterparts; they shared similar problems. Others may have looked for a calmer atmosphere where historical stereotypes of one community towards the other would be secondary.

Statistically, intermarriages of this kind show that couples occupy a middle point between an overly religious and exclusive tradition, and a too-liberal one. They involve partners who feel that ultimately their intermarriage may be manageable, often within a context of 'modified patriarchy', without slipping into serious problems.

Differences in the bereavement patterns and rituals between various religious communities occupy a central role in highlighting conflicts (Ata, 1994).

Assessing the nature and extent of unhappiness in marriage with accuracy is a difficult. The research can elicit information about marital adjustment, companionship and conflicts.

Although the group under investigation escaped the arranged marriages that occurred in the 1980s, they seemed to encounter different kinds of pressures. The community's unwritten declaration of non-interference in securing

Table 9.3
Positive Features

Q: Your partner's religion is different from yours. What do you like least about this?		Q: You have a mixed Muslim–Christian marriage. What do you like least about it?	
No answer	34%	No answer	28%
Incompatibility of backgrounds, conflicts, pressures, obligations, mistrust, dogma	21%	Incompatibility of backgrounds, conflicts, pressures, obligations, mistrust, dogma	33%
Apathy; absence of religion, bonding and sense of sharing celebrations and common activities; children's uncertainty	11%	Apathy; absence of religion, bonding and sense of sharing celebrations and common activities; children's uncertainty	16%
Don't know	27%	Don't know	23%
Meaningless answers	7%	Meaningless answers	0%

the wife's rights following the wedding may still hold, although to a lesser degree. An open-ended question was posed to couples in order to elicit information of this nature. Tables 9.3 and 9.4 list their responses.

A sizeable percentage of the responses relate to pressures triggered by the one's social background, as conditioned by affiliation to a religious and cultural community. A total of 20 individuals (approximately 21%) perceived that their married life was made unpleasant, at least in part, by outside forces, including their immediate religious community, family and friends, and the wider community. The figure swells to 33% when the question focused on Christian/Muslim marriages in general. This contrasts with 11% and 16% (for responses on their own situation and in general) who attributed unpleasant-

Table 9.4
Positive Features

Q: Your partner's religion is different from yours. What do you like most about this?		Q: You have mixed Muslim–Christian marriage. What do you like most about this?	
Exposure to new culture, ideas and perspectives on life, compromise and forgiveness	28%	Exposure, understanding, tolerance, compromise, acceptance, and empathy	55%
Other general comments including religion is not relevant, food, commitment, spouse converted to 'my religion'	43%	Departure from religious adherence, secular living and independence	16%
Don't care or don't know	28%	Both religions are similar, no difference between them	25%
Not applicable	1%	Absolutely nothing	4%

ness to an absence of shared activity, common purpose of living and aspirations as a unified household.

Several participants who indicated that there were no differences added that their parents did not approve of their marriage because their grandchildren might become exclusively Christian or Muslim.

The largest group, approximately one-third, declined to provide any answers relating to this question.

Fearing that interreligious marriages may shake the community from which they draw their support, some ethnic Christian religious leaders have voiced concern about the growing vulnerability of the family, attributed mainly to the mass media in general and mixed marriages in particular. A Melbourne-based community leader cautions:

> Mixed [inter-religious] marriages effect many harmful situations and dissent between couples. It is not easy for their parents to turn a blind eye to their marrying son or daughter converting to each other's religion. This will lead to a household of evil, one which produces tension and hatred; subsequently ending in destruction including children. Adding to that, a Christian woman will not accept polygamy or divorce as non-Christians do. The slightest disagreements may lead to divorce.
>
> Our advice to Christian women is to persevere in their religion, resisting all short-lived seductions resulting in intractable crises. As regards our men, holding on to their religion and high moral ground will set a good example for men from other religions to follow (Yacoub, 1981).

Similar concerns were voiced in research conducted in other countries, as Stilyana (1997) notes:

> The conclusions I could draw ... are that both Christian and Muslim communities take marriage between individuals with different religious background for something unnatural. The fear of the mixed marriage is the fear of eventual conflict that will have consequences for both sides. To put it in a different way — the mixed marriage is not the preferred form for either group While mixed marriages do exist and are based upon the free choice of the partners, they are confronted with strong negative reactions — by the parents on both sides, by the respective kin groups, and by the surrounding religious communities. (p. 5)

The general rule is the same as it has always been: a Christian woman is to marry a Christian man. However, if a minor difference exists between two Christian denominations, let the church then allow the Catholic woman (or man) to intermarry, providing he or she takes an oath to preserve their religious obligations, with the consent of their future spouse.

If the groom-to-be is not Christian, the church may demand freedom of worship, upbringing of children, unity of marriage, rights of inheritance, and so on. These conditions are not made available to the Christian woman upon her marriage to a Muslim, and therefore the church does not sanction these kind of marriages. There is no guarantee of her religious freedom, freedom in the upbringing of her children, nor the commitment by her husband that he won't marry another woman at the same time.

In the end she would be placed under enormous social pressure, particularly if her children deny their Christian faith. Who can possibly contemplate that their daughter marries solely to satisfy her desire or her spouse's?

The problems outlined above are community related, suggesting the continuing strength of, and pressure from, traditional ties, and are not due to problems associated, say, with shared decision-making. These problems also seem to rank higher than factors such as economic difficulties, lack of freedom of movement or the burden of bringing up children.

A psychological instrument to explore more deeply the nature of such responses is needed.

These responses contrast with those obtained during the 1980s study. In the earlier study, most of the complaints were directed at husbands' lack of interaction, coming from their belief in the separation of the sexes. Wives in that study complained about the excessive freedom of their husbands compared to the little freedom they were given. In the current study there was no mention of this.

In both studies, pressures from the surrounding community were identified, but for different reasons. In the former study, obligations towards relatives and the larger family network were mentioned as a main source of unpleasantness, whereas in this study it is the undeserved stigma and lukewarm behaviour that disrupt their relationship.

This is not surprising, given the relatively free environment that Australian culture provides in which male–female relationships can develop.

There was little concern about the future of children and the problems associated with their acceptance and identity. Specific uneasy feelings are mentioned below. Approximately 1% of interviewees gave answers that were too remote from the subject matter. The following statements are examples of each of the above:

Apathy
He [my son] doesn't know what [he] really is. He feels he belongs to both religions. There is no support from anyone around, about their well-being, and at school it is like a different place altogether.

The society doesn't agree with this. Our kids have already mental insecurity. What kinds of problems will they face when they grow up? Right now they have been to church ... Next time to the mosque. And no one asks questions about them going only to this or that place.

Reactions from relatives or friends
My parents ... were angry because their daughters marry into the other religion. They make them feel like strangers. There is total displeasure from everyone, especially when differences [conflicts] take place. It is as if they feel justified. They say, didn't we warn them all the time?

Reactions from the community
Most of the [community] do not like it. They look at us in a condescending way. Some do but after they do a lot of adjustment. We change and our children develop new things, and customs, and so we will never adapt completely. Besides, there are no open-minded people within our community to make friends with.

Disapproval from one's own religious community
It's the attitudes of Christians towards people like my wife. They don't want to know her or have any relationship with her because they think she was forced to change her religion. She got ex-communicated and she is not happy about that. They only hear the gossip ...
It's all because of fanaticism. Each religion [religious community] wants to draw the children to them. This is nature. You just can not go against it or change it.

Incompatibility of cultural and/or religious background
One's freedom is gone. Just like that, especially if she is a female Christian. She can move by herself, and all their eyes will be on her [in Arabic kul eyunhum aleha].
The marriage will not be 100% perfect. Sometimes we agree but not always, especially when we cannot come to an understanding.

Such responses are common among married couples, yet for those outside this kind of relationship, common heritage and the sharing of concerns are important in the struggle for national liberation. Those who espouse such views include Esposito (1997, p. 36) who says,

> ... despite important differences of belief and practice, there is shared heritage of faith and value: belief in God, the prophets, revelation, moral responsibility and accountability, divine reward and punishment, and social justice can be a strong source of mutual respect and co-operation.

The survival of a Christian minority within a Muslim community may be dependent on the strengthening of mutual understanding between the two communities and the forging of a national-type alliance. How much of this will be needed to survive marital discord is difficult to estimate.

Making a conscientious decision to intermarry in the face of various cultural stigmas does not make life easy or even tolerable. This is evident from the figures above. Almost 16% of the group felt that interreligious marriages were worse than marriages of the same religion. Unanticipated expectations of managing unforeseen difficulties could be a key factor. Unable to find religious or cultural support, this group offers advice to future generations; both individuals and society may not be prepared to accommodate them comfortably as full members.

Positive features of Christian–Muslim marriages

Fulfilling one's aspirations of bearing children soon after marriage is a highly prized attribute, not only for women but also for the extended family, neighbours, friends and the community. The importance of this is not to be trivialised. Gadallah, (1977, p. 328) makes this point clear:

> The fear of being a 'barren' woman is not eliminated until the first pregnancy has occurred. From month to month after marriage, the new bride hopes and prays that she does not menstruate, for she has been told that missing the menstrual period is a sign of pregnancy. The eagerness of the bride's parents, husband and in-laws for this sign is not any less than that of the bride herself, for all of them are anxious to see that the bride is not barren.

As one would expect, the responses to this question were so varied that they had to be aggregated. The fact that half of this group (55%) indicated responses such as cultural exposure and religious tolerance, reduction of hatred between the two communities, love, understanding and liberal lifestyle, and relationships, is a promising sign. There is a clear-cut emphasis on family relationships and transcending traditional expectations. The previous study showed that 29% believed having children was the most positive thing about their marriage; however, this group failed to rate this factor at all.

It is a worry that a handful of participants found no positive features in their marriage. Speculation on why people gave no response (4%) towards mixed marriages in general or towards their own (28%) is left to the reader.

Select statements from the above categories are listed below:

> *Cultural exposure and tolerance*
> These marriages make the bond between them stronger. I know nothing about the other [Christian] religion for the first time. It is good. It makes people convert from a world of darkness into a world of enlightenment. You begin to see how the other people live and that makes you more tolerant ... It also removes barriers between religious and cultural communities, and melts the difference, lessens the tension and fanatic behaviours.

> *Exposure, understanding and liberal life at home*
> It creates an opportunity to seek each other's opinion. This will remove barriers between both religions. It [marriage] is good as long as it is built on understanding. For me it was a chance to learn more about

Christianity and a great opportunity to bridge the gap of suspicion between the two religions. The difficulty though is to come to terms with all the opposing views.

It takes hard work and commitment, but it takes us out of out limited worlds. This is crazy because the rest of the community cannot open up to the difference. And therefore the couples must be educated so that their marriage will be complete and successful.

Support from the family
My husband's family were with us all the time. No signs of disapproval, no nothing. Everyone knows a bit about each other's beliefs. All my children are Christians and accepted by [my] husband's community.

Other general comments
It depends how people manage their relationship.

For her [the bride] to convert into her husband's religion everything will be OK.

Marriage is a matter of fate. Traditional marriages are not ideal.

People with mixed marriages identify more with Australia and less so with their religion.

It is less expensive, particularly if the wife is foreigner.

It is cool. It is the real thing. I worship my God and he worships his. Never thought about it really.

Religion is no measure of friendship. I have many friends, and this will bring people closer to each other than religion. Also, if the wife accepts her husband's religion all problems will disappear.

No positive features
Just write down nothing. No comment. The fact that we argue over religious issues and how to bring up our children makes me wonder that I should have married from the same religion. When we got married, religion was no big deal. Now [we are older] it is important, just like that.

Conclusions

One conclusion is that this group had few illusions about marriage, and were frank about their feelings. References to polarisation of roles were minor, signifying an increased effort by partners to deal with the strains created by those around them. Frustration naturally comes with new changes, with increased awareness and availability of options.

Several members displayed distinctive attitudes towards the family, divorce and the marital relationship. Evidence that heterogamous couples will be more likely to divorce than those who share similar characteristics does not carry weight. The homogamy theory could apply to those who differ in age, religion, education and ethnic origin, in that they are likely to experience greater marital conflict and higher rates of marital breakdown than other couples (Jones, 1994). For this sample the major difference between couples has been religion.

It will be interesting to follow this group, to be able to provide clearer predictions for future generations. It was found that marrying into a group with a low propensity for divorce tends to reduce the risk of divorce for a partner originating from a high divorce group.

Even so, the majority has indicated a kind of attitudinal change after marriage in accommodating facets of their upbringing into the frame of their relationship. Others have attempted, by their own volition, to convert to the religion of their spouse.

It is obvious that there are several ways to deal with religious and cultural differences. These include integrating each of the spouse's expectations, adopting some of the approaches of the partner, isolation or apathy, and abstaining from sharing.

Cultural background and religious affiliation have strong influence over the individual's health, adjustment and overall well-being (Ata, 1986). For example, in Muslim groups, unrestrained emotional expression in public towards loss is strongly encouraged, as compared to Australian-born and other Christian migrants. This indicates that those who are religiously oriented exhibit lower anxiety symptoms in dealing with loss traumas.

Those who believe that adjustments in behaviour are not easy to identify or observe contend that they mostly take place in private. Penny and Khoo (1996, p. 26) note that

> ... in some aspects of their lives a couple may adopt Australian behavioural norms, in others, those of the migrant partner. Some couples may take another approach, called 'the third space', in which individuals are freed of some cultural constraints and allowed the creation of cultural identity on an individual level.

References

Al-Ghazali. (n.d.) *The confessions of Al-Ghazali* (Claude Field, Trans.). Lahore, Ashraf.

Ata, A.W. (1980). *The Lebanese community in Melbourne: Ethnicity and acculturation.* Unpublished doctoral dissertation, University of Melbourne, Australia.

Ata, A.W. (1986). *The West Bank Palestinian family.* London: Kegan Paul International.

Ata, A.W. (1994). *Bereavement and health: Gender, religious, psychological and cross cultural issues.* Melbourne: David Lovell Publishing.

Ata, A.W. (2000). *Intermarriage between Christians and Muslims: A West Bank study.* Melbourne: David Lovell Publishing.

Bajeva, M. (1981). *Women in Islam.* New York: Advent Books.

Birrell, B. (1995). Spouse migration to Australia. *People and Place, 3*(1), 9–16.

Birrell, B., & Healy, E. (2000). Out-marriage and the survival of ethnic communities in Australia. *People and Place, 8*(3), 37–46.

Blau, P., Blum, T., & Schwartz, J. (1982). Heterogeneity and intermarriage. *American Sociological Review, 47*, 45–62.

Esposito, J. (1997). Christian–Muslim relations in historic perspective. In N. Ateek. (Ed.), *Jerusalem: What makes for peace?* (pp. 31–37). London: Milesende.

Gadallah, S. (1977). The influence of reproductive norms in family size and fertility behaviours. In S. Ibrahim (Ed.), *Arab society in transition* (pp. 106–122). Cairo: American University Press.

Jones, F. (1994). Are marriages that cross ethnic boundaries more likely to end in divorce? *Journal of Australian Population Association, 11*(2), 115–131.

Penny, J., & Khoo, S.-E. (1996). *Intermarriage: A study of migration and integration.* Canberra, Australia: Australian Government Printing Service.

Price, C. (1993). Ethnic intermixture in Australia. *People and Place, 1*(1), 6–8.

Yacoub, A. (1981). *Marriage and the divorce in history.* Melbourne, Australia: St George Orthodox Church.

Bibliography

Adams, B. (1986). *The family: A sociological interpretation.* New York: Harcourt, Brace Jovanovich.

Al-Haj, M. (1983). *Family lifestyles in an Arab town in Israel.* Unpublished doctoral dissertation, Hebrew University, Jerusalem.

Al-Haj, M. (1988). The changing Arab kinship structure: The effect of modernization in an urban community. *Economic Development and Cultural Change, 36*(2), 237–258.

Ata, A.W. (1980). Marriage patterns among the Lebanese community in Melbourne. *Australian and New Zealand Journal of Sociology, 16*(3), 112–113.

Ata, A.W. (1981). Prospects and retrospects on the role of Muslim Arab women at present: Trends and tendencies. *Islamic Culture, 55*(4) pp 259-276.

Ata, A.W. (1984). Impact of westernization, and other forces, on the status of Muslim women in the Arab Middle East. *The Eastern Anthropologist, 37*(2), 95–126.

Ata, A.W. (1988–1990). *Religion and ethnic identity* (Vols. 1–3). Melbourne, Australia: Spectrum Publications.

Ateeq, N. (Ed.), Duaybis, C., & Schrader, M. (1997). *Jerusalem: What makes for peace?* London: Milesende.

Avruch, K., & Blackk, P. (1993). Conflict resolution in inter-cultural settings: Problems and prospects. In D. Sandole & H. Van der Merwe (Eds.), *Conflict resolution theory and practice: Integration and application.* New York: St Martin's Press.

Beck, U. (1999). *World risk society.* Cambridge: Polity Press.

Betts, R. (1978). *Christians in the Arab east.* Atlanta: John Knox Press.

Birrell, B. (1995). Spouse migration to Australia. *People and Place, 3*(1), 9–16.

Bouma, G. (1994). *Mosques and Muslim settlement in Australia.* Canberra, Australia: Australian Government Publishing Service.

Esposito, J. (1999). *The Islamic threat: Myth or reality?* (3rd ed.). New York: Oxford University Press.

Gariano, A. (1994). Religious identification and marriage. *People and Place, 2*(1), 41–47.

Gariano, A., & Rutland, D. (1997). Religious Intermix: 1996 census update. *People and Place*, 5(4), 14.

Goodnow, J., & Cashmore, J. (1985). Parents expectations in some Australian groups: cultural differences. In M. Poole & P. deLacey (Eds.), *Australia in transition: Culture and life possibilities* (pp. 233–244). Sydney, Australia: Harcourt Brace Jovanovich.

Gray, A. (1987). Intermarriage, opportunity and preference. *Population Studies, 41*, 365–379.

Gray, A. (1989). Measuring preference in intermarriage: a response to McCaa. *Population Studies*, 43(1), 163–166.

Hanson, V. (2002). Why the Muslims misjudged us. *City-Journal, 12*(1), 8.

Price, C. (1988/1999). The melting pot is working. *IPA Review, 2*(3), 34–35.

Price, C. (1994). Ethnic intermixture in Australia. *People and Place, 2*(4), 8–11.

Price, C., & Zubrzycki, J. (1962). The use of intermarriage statistics as an index of intermarriage. *Population Studies, 15,* 58–69.

Prior, M., & Taylor, W. (Eds.). (1994). *Christians in the holy land*. London: The World of Islam Trust Publishers.

Raheb, M. (1995). *I am a Palestinian Christian*. Minneapolis, MN: Fortress Press.

Stevens, G. (1985). Nativity, intermarriage and mother tongue shift. *American Sociological Review, 50,* 74–83.

Stephan, C., & Stephan, W. (1989). After intermarriage: Ethnic identity among mixed-heritage. *Journal of Marriage and Family, 51*(2), 507–551.

Stewart, N. (1966). Global Christian theology and education. In J. Ashley & L. Francis (Eds.), *Christian theology and religious education: Connections and contradictions*. London: Society for Promoting Christian Knowledge.

Stilyana M. (l997) *Mixed marriages between Bulgarians and Bulgarian Muslims: An undesirable event*. University of Sofia, Bulgaria. Available at http://www.cit.bg/home/bsrcs/mixed.htm

Storer, D. (1985). *Ethnic family values in Australia*. Sydney, Australia: Prentice Hall.

Chapter 10

Bereavement Anxieties and Health
Among the Arab Muslim Community

Religious and cultural diversity in Australia has been overlooked by many religious, educational, and health care institutions where practices and attitudes to death and bereavement are concerned. The formation of culturally appropriate treatment plans necessitates a radical turnabout, namely adjusting one's perception and awareness to different cultural and religious values. Likewise, the need to develop culturally diverse health services is important. This chapter describes the shortcomings of the mental health model of Western cultures, such as in Australia, where members of a community are no longer homogeneous within their cultural and religious backgrounds. In a multicultural society, where the basis of understanding traumas and stress is interconnected with religious and cultural undercurrents, myopic psychiatry and health approaches are rendered ineffective. Suggestions are offered to how better address the needs of people from culturally and linguistically diverse backgrounds.

Western psychiatry has developed as an ethnocentric discipline with illness as a basis for its model — a rationale that took precedence over anthropological considerations. In disregarding the presence of other racial and cultural perspectives, Western health-care institutions, of which psychiatry is a frontrunner, failed to rid itself of culturally distorted perspectives and sensitivities regarding non-European, non-American communities. What constitutes the foundations of Western psychiatry and its rational scientific approach are cultural assumptions where individual, material and non-religious interests dominate. The result is a hierarchical order of human values that is fundamentally at odds with non-Western psychiatry.

In the case of mourning rituals and ceremonies surrounding death, there are vast differences between the two systems in terms of overall diagnosis and healing assumptions. Where rituals involving a dynamic relationship between the grieving process and support providers, as healing powers in traditional spiritually oriented societies, Western psychiatry dismisses these as irrelevant to its biomedical treatment methods. For example, culturally sanctioned expressions that are considered by many migrant communities as coping strategies, including passivity, euphoria, aggression, submissiveness, extroversion, self-flagellation, non-assertiveness, psychological martyrdom, hierarchical dependence, hearing voices, masculinity, and femininity, are often described by Western psychiatry as pathologies.

The study presented in this chapter draws on the emotional experiences of bereaved Muslims, and presents them as the bereaved themselves interpret them. Often their reactions and impressions told us about things we were not looking for, or would have dismissed as peripheral. The result is a text that is experience-based in content, yet within a theoretical framework. It avoids the drawbacks of remote abstraction and theory.

Aims and Significance of this Research

The study specifically examines the health, religious, ethnic, gender, age and psychological dimensions of bereavement.

It provides mechanisms for health care workers that might open communication between the bereaved and the dying, the family and staff members, and that might encourage them to view death in a less negative way so that feelings of adjustment will ensue. It also promotes the understanding of the dynamic of cross-religious and cross-cultural grief.

Method

A sample size of 30 households in Shepparton, Albury-Wodonga, and Melbourne were set as a target for the survey research. Although small, the number was chosen as being sufficiently flexible to permit statistical reliability, cross-tabulation of variables, and measurement of mean scores. Seven other religious and ethnic groups consisting of 239 households took part in the survey for the purpose of cross-comparative analysis. The distribution of these categories is set out in Table 10.1.

Addresses of participants were canvassed from select ethnic and religious leaders. Participants in the study were 18 years and older. Where possible the closest person to the deceased was requested to participate, or alternatively another member of the family. The period of loss should not have exceeded 5

Table 10.1
Religion–Cultural Distribution

Religious and ethnic groups	No.	%
Australian-born Christians (self and parents)	62	23.1%
Irish-born Catholics	28	10.4%
Arab-born Muslims	30	11.2%
Vietnamese-born Buddhists	27	10.0%
Indian-born Hindus–Sikhs	31	11.5%
Other Christian migrants	66	24.5%
Other minor religions	18	6.7%
Non-religious affiliates	7	2.6%
Total	269	100%

years for the interviewee. The interview was conducted in English so as to avoid potential discrepancies in meaning between languages.

Findings

Emotions of grief

The impact of religious affiliation and cultural upbringing on bereavement and health vary in intensity and form. For example, findings in Figure 10.1 show that unrestrained emotional expression is encouraged in one community group but is strongly discouraged in another. The level of significance ($p = .003$) indicates that significant variation exists among the various groups on 'feeling ashamed at public expressions of grief', with the Muslims ranking highest and the Hindus–Sikhs, Other Minor Religions and Non-religious affiliates lowest.

For comparative purposes, other possible differences regarding the issue of 'feeling of shame at public expression of grief were examined according to the variables pertaining to gender, age and education (see Figure 10.2). Measures of significance on the chi square test did not reveal statistical difference among the three age groups ($p = .5$) nor between different levels of education ($p = .7$). However, a strong relationship was found on the gender variable ($p = .002$), showing that the proportion of males (23%) experiencing feelings of shame at a public expression of grief was almost three times higher than that of females (9%).

The resolution of grief of first generation Muslim migrants (i.e., those born outside Australia) is interconnected with their adaptive and acculturation process as much as to the affiliation to their ethnic community. Clearly, their emotional ties with their home town and relatives whom they left behind have not been totally severed. Not being able to view the body of a deceased relative nor to participate in deeply cherished elaborate mourning ceremonies as in the old country is both painful and guilt evoking. Their guilt feelings are further multiplied in believing that they have let down the mourner relatives in their home country by not being around during the funeral.

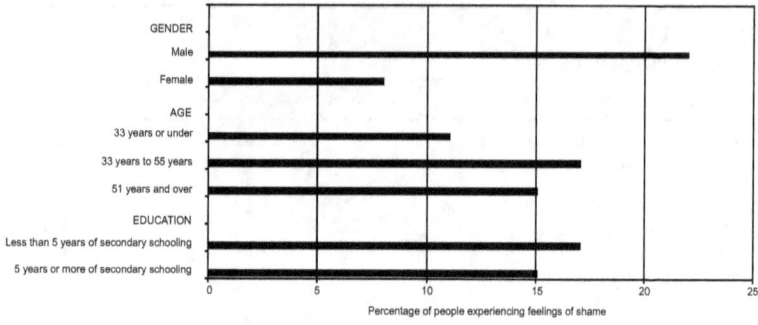

Figure 10.1
Feelings of shame at public expression of grief, by gender, by age and by education.

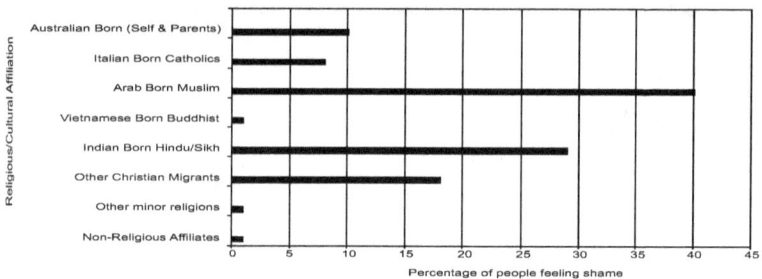

Figure 10.2
Feelings of shame at public expression of grief, by religion/culture.

It is also reasoned that because first generation immigrants descend from certain ethnic or religious backgrounds their grief behaviour is immediately expected to fit into specific patterns that have been transplanted by leaders of ethnic communities in a multicultural society like Australia (Ata, 1988, 1989, 1990).

It has been shown that first generation immigrants are particularly vulnerable to burdensome grief emotions. They may not have support for their grieving periods in the host country. A case in point is a bereaved migrant family that became quite distressed about not being able to afford to go to view the body of a deceased relative in the old country.

Religious affiliation and death anxiety

The relationship between Islam and death anxiety is significant. Perspectives on the implications of such a relationship have been discussed by several theorists (Leming, 1990). Islam functions as a unifying force for disrupting and

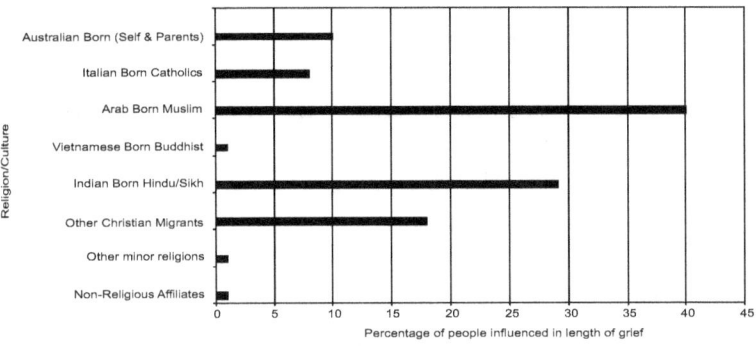

Figure 10.3
Length of grieving by religion/culture.

upsetting events that interfere with routine life events and their continuity. In making worshippers aware of human anxieties, of which death anxiety is a major one, religious institutions provide a sense of cohesion and common concern.

Tests were carried out on the strength of these relationships. They indicate, for example, that the relationship between the length of grieving reported by the various sample groups, and their belonging to their ethnic or religious communities is strong, according to chi-square and Lambda tests (see Figure 10.3). The overall response is high, the lowest provided by Non-religious affiliate (38%) and the highest provided by Arab-born Muslims and Vietnamese-born Buddhists (both 80%).

The findings shown in Figure 10.4 reveal a diversity of responses about experiencing more manageable grieving conditions because of the respondents' affiliation to their own religious or ethnic community. According to the t test, the relationship between religious or ethnic affiliation and a feeling of an improved grieving condition is not the result of a chance factor; it indicates causality (although the statistical differences between the various religious or cultural groups was weak, that is, lower than 20% according to the Lambda measure of significance).

Leading in the response that religious or cultural affiliation creates a better grieving condition is the Muslim group (96.7%), followed by Other Minor Religions (83.3%) and Vietnamese-born Buddhists (65.4%).

In another recent study a similar curvilinear relationship was found between death anxieties and religiosity variables (Leming, 1990). High- and low-rating religious people were found to have a low degree of anxiety whereas moderately committed people show a high degree of it.

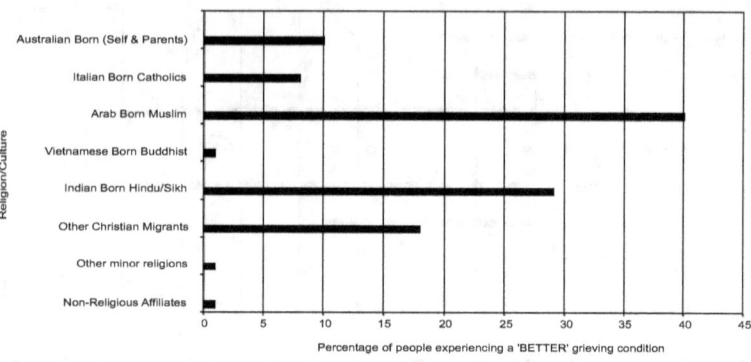

Figure 10.4
Grieving condition, by religious/cultural affiliation.

Hollingsworth (1977) and others note that Islam focuses on the tenuous nature of life and respect for the dead. The belief that we all are created by God and should return to God is the basis for this focus. Islam provides graphic descriptions of heaven and hell. The perception that death is a necessary gateway to eternity for both the soul and the body is equally shared by Christians.

Cultural differences in funeral practices and emotional expressions

Every culture has deeply entrenched traditional customs of handling death as grief ensues. Societal-based reactions become more pronounced in the form of funeral practices (Figure 10.5).

Of interest are the Arab-born Muslims who registered the lowest response (27%) of reported differences between their country of birth and Australia's funeral practices, even though the differences are ostensibly as great as those reported by the other five groups.

No statistical difference emerged between the gender groups ($p = .55$); education groups ($p = .15$), or among the three age groups ($p = .66$) in the chi-square t test (see Figure 10.3). Comments and reactions by individuals were unique and in ample supply. The following direct quotes were selected from a bereaved father:

> Where I come from there are no funeral directors. It is at the family's level with all the near and dear ones. They have become more formal in Australia — a really very tense time. Expenses here are greater. We hire cars to take us to the cemetery; in Italy we walk carrying the coffin on our shoulder. The body would be kept at home for 24 hours while the relatives stayed and grieved. In Australia funerals are more ostentatious; people go to the pub instead of having supper together. People here wear lively colours and patterns to funerals, and women don't wear

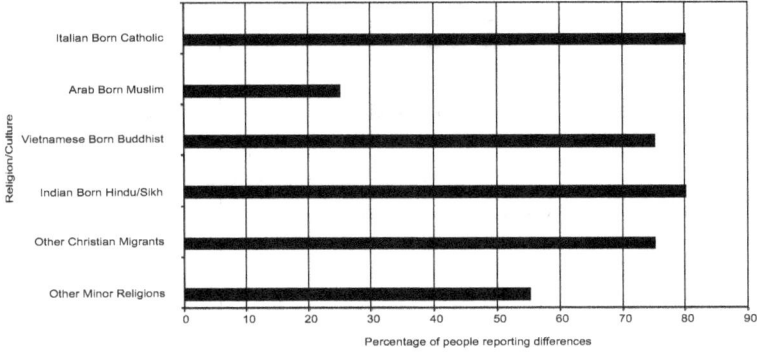

Figure 10.5
Reported differences between country of birth and Australia's funeral practices, by religion/culture.

veils. There is less respect shown. Funeral directors tell people who attend the funeral to leave the cemetery after the service is over. I do want to stay longer sometimes.

Participants indicated a range of physical and emotional expressions that they recall having experienced in public at the funeral.

Reactions such as beating the breast, pulling hair, slapping one's head, wailing in unison, fainting and injuring oneself registered a smaller response than weeping and restraining oneself from showing emotions.

In particular, weeping drew the largest reported emotional expression by all groups except the Arab-born Muslims. The disproportionate representation of male and females may have contributed to this, particularly as weeping in public by males is discordant with the main cultural values.

In restraining oneself from showing emotions, the Australian-born group registered the highest response (74%), followed by Indian-born Sikhs and Hindus (61%). Other Minor Religions registered the lowest response (2%).

Communicating with the deceased

The need for communication is universal among human beings. This need may become intense when getting together with others is not possible. To many of the bereaved, opting to be comforted by the illusion of the presence of the deceased is a lesser trauma than facing the pain of death. It provides an escape from the anguish of finality; the hope of permanence overrides the despair of extinction.

Differences across religious and cultural groups with regards to the appearance of the deceased are shown in Figure 10.6. A high percentage of Muslims

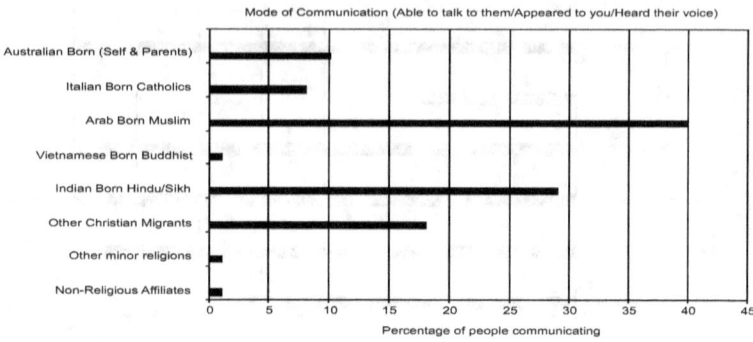

Figure 10.6
Communication with the deceased, by religion/culture.

(63.3%) and Hindu–Sikhs (40.9%) reported seeing their dead loved ones at some stage after the funeral. A smaller percentage from the other groups also reported a similar experience, excluding those without any religion.

Figure 10.6 shows an aggregate (i.e., combined) response of three modes of communication with the deceased. When analysed separately, a sharper difference emerges between the groups. For example, the response to hearing voices of the deceased is slightly different, although a similar pattern is observed across the seven religious communities. Fifty per cent of Muslims and 36% of Italian Catholics reported hearing the voices of their deceased.

Statistical differences among the various groups on the variables of 'attempting to talk to, or hearing voices, were non-significant. However, a high level of statistical difference ($p = .01$) was found to exist among the various groups on the variable 'Appearing to you', with Australian-born respondents ranking lowest (13.5%) and Arab-born Muslims ranking highest (63.3%).

Significantly, some psychiatrists believe that speaking to the dead is not the same as seeing ghosts or hearing voices, and that many people may speak to the dead even though they may believe no one is actually listening. In my analysis, such argument holds as much weight as its opposite. If one continues to speak to the dead in the same manner as if they were not, the boundaries to hallucination ipso facto are not significantly different to hearing or seeing ghosts.

Almost half of the female sample (49.7%) and just over one-third of the males (39%) reported having attempted to talk to their deceased. A similar discrepancy emerged with regard to hearing their voices and the deceased appearing to them. However, the differences between the gender groups are significant ($p = .04$) only in the first communication category.

The gender issue is interesting in that it evokes a number of possible explanations. First, the volume of emotional investment and depth of feelings in relationships is known to be more characteristic for females than males. It is also suggested that women view an intimate close relationship as more important for good mental health and high morale than occupational or social status. The small body of literature in psychology is filled with studies on the relatively marked intensity of relationships and depth of introspection as expressed by women (Gething, 1989).

Summary and Conclusions

The general picture that emerges from analysis of the data in this project is somewhat daunting and yet provides information that is relevant to mental and other health care providers in considering the relationship between wellbeing, health and bereavement.

Cultural background and religious affiliation have been found to be strong indicators of the individual's health and overall wellbeing.

The relationship between religious affiliation and death anxiety was found to be a strong one. It was found, for example, that a relationship between the length of grieving as reported by the various groups in this study and their belonging to their ethnic or religious communities is statistically high. Leading in these responses is the Muslim group (96.7%), followed by Other Minor Religions (83.35%) and Buddhist Vietnamese (65.4%).

Affiliation to a religion seems to provide the bereaved with great strength and sustenance in their dealing with death. For example, in Muslim community groups, unrestrained emotional expression in public towards loss is strongly encouraged, as compared to Australian-born, Italian-born, Vietnamese-born and other Christian migrants ($p = .003$). These findings, however, should in no way suggest psychological deprivation or absence of wellbeing for those without religious affiliation.

Significant differences were revealed between the sexes on such matters as health problems, grief expressions, psychosomatic manifestations, communication with the dead, beliefs in the afterlife and interpretation of the meaning of loss.

One of the strong differences between the sexes related to the feeling of shame at public expression of grief ($p = .002$). The findings reveal that the proportion of males (23%) was almost three times higher in experiencing feelings of shame at public expression of grief than females (9%).

Another finding showed that almost half of the females sampled (49.7%), compared to just over one-third of the males (39%), reported having attempted to talk to the deceased. A similar discrepancy emerged with regard to hearing their voices and the deceased appearing to them.

The gender issue is interesting in that it raises a number of possible explanations. First, the volume of emotional investment and depth of feeling in relationships is known to be more characteristic for females than males. It also suggests that women view an intimate close relationship as more important for good mental health and high morale than occupational or social status.

For Western psychiatry, the model of mental health may be considered beneficial in direct proportion to the extent to which it is influenced by members of the culture it hopes to treat. That is, it can be considered as useful as it is sensitive and open to diverse cultures. However, in a multicultural society, where the basis of understanding trauma and stress is interconnected with religious and spiritual undercurrents, Western-style psychiatry is rendered ineffective as far as it is 'in itself' and 'for itself'. In other words, because it carries with it the assumption of superiority, it will not be open to integrating approaches that others regard as effective.

The assumption that what is diagnosed in Euro–American cultures as psychopathological must by necessity be universal, is not only indicative of myopic vision but also evokes dissatisfaction among other cultures. Western psychiatry cannot assume a universally established context from which it can deal with culturally conditioned fears, or a variety of other feelings and behaviours. Western psychiatry has a duty to grow within our postmodern world to a maturity in which difference and otherness are encountered with wisdom, service, and a heart.

It is recommended that the relationship between the treatment of bereavement-associated pathologies, the bereaved premigration experience, and cultural upbringing, be further explored. This will provide mechanisms for health care providers to openly communication with the patient, the family and staff members. It will also provide information for specialised counselling and correct intervention as required.

The ability to recognise and interpret expressions of bereavement specific to Muslim communities may result in cost-effective community and health services for families.

References

Ata, A. (1986). Cultural pluralism, ethnocentricity and inter-ethnic relationships. *Eastern Anthropologist, 39*(4).

Ata, A. (1988–1990). *Religion and ethnic identity: An Australian study* (Vols. I–III). Melbourne, Australia: Spectrum Publications.

Ata, A., Klimidis, S., & Minas, H. (1992). The PBI-BC: A brief current form of the parental bonding instrument for adolescent research. *Comprehensive Psychiatry, 33*(6), 374–377.

Eisenbruch, M. (1984). Cross-cultural aspects of bereavement II: Ethnic and cultural variations in development of bereavement practices. *Culture, Medicine and Psychiatry, 8*, 315–347.

Ferguson, B., & Browne, M.E. (1991). *Health care and immigrants*. Sydney, Australia: MacLennan and Petty.

Gatrad, A.R., & Sheikh, A. (Eds.). (2000). *Caring for Muslim patients*. England: Radcliffe Medical Press Ltd.

Gething, L. (1984). *Lifespan and human development*. New York: McGraw Hill.

Gonda, T., & Ruark, J. (1984). *Dying dignified: The health professional's guide to care*. London: Addison-Wesley.

Graham, H. (1986). *The human face of psychology: Humanistic psychology in its historical, social and cultural contexts*. Milton Keynes: Open University Press.

Holland, K., & Hogg, C. (2001). *Cultural awareness in nursing and health care: An introductory text*. London: Arnold.

Hollingsworth, C., & Pasnau, R. (1977). *The family in mourning*. New York: Grune and Stratton.

Kalish, R. (1981). *Death, grief and caring relationships*. Monterey: Brooks/Cole.

Kinzie, J., Tran, K., & Bloom, J. (1980). An Indo-Chinese refugee psychiatric clinic: Culturally accepted treatment approaches. *American Journal of Psychiatry, 137*, 1429–1432.

Leming, M. (1990). *Understanding dying, death, and bereavement*. Fort Worth: Holt.

Littlewood, J. (1983). *Loss and change: a consideration for death related issues*. Unpublished doctoral dissertation, University of Leicester, United Kingdom.

Littlewood, J. (1992). *Aspects of grief: Bereavement in adult life*. London: Tavistock/Routledge.

Marris, P. (1986). *Loss and change*. London: Routledge Kegan and Paul.

Rahim, A., & Mukherjee, A. (1984). *South Asians in transition: Problems and challenges*. Scarborough: Indian Immigrant Aid Services.

Rando, T. (1984). *Grief, dying and death: Clinical interpretations for caregivers*. Champaign: Research Press Company.

Raphael, B., & Singh, B. (1981). Post-disaster morbidity of the bereaved. *Journal of Nervous and Mental Disease, 169*(4), 208–212.

Redi, J., & Strong, T. (1987). *Torture and trauma: The health care needs of refugee victims in New South Wales*. Sydney, Australia: Cumberland College of Health Services.

Reich, P., DeSilva, R., Lown, B., & Murawski, B. (1983). Acute psychological disturbance preceding life-threatening ventricular arrythmias. *Journal of the American Medical Association, 250*, 374–399.

Reid, J., & Trompf, P. (Eds.). (1990). *The health of immigrant Australia: A social perspective*. Sydney, Australia: Harcourt Brace Jovanovich.

Schofield, T. (1990). Living with disability. In J. Reid & P. Trompf (Eds.), *The health of immigrant Australia: A social perspective*. Sydney, Australia: Harcourt Brace Jovanovich.

Shuchter, S. (1986). *Dimensions of grief: Adjusting to the death of a spouse*. London: Jossey-Bass.

Chapter 11

Observing Different Faiths, Learning About Ourselves
Practice With Intermarried Muslims and Christians*

Generalising About 'Them'

When you hear someone say 'he's a typical Pom' you know that the person being discussed is not properly represented by this statement. Goldstein (1983, p. 267) argued that stereotyping clients on the basis of their cultural background fails to 'start where this client is'. Thus, even as one might professionally think it is appropriate to focus on a particular difference, there are risks when the notion of culture (or indeed any other key signifier) is invoked, as this can inadvertently objectify what is not intended. As Said (1978) and other postcolonial theorists argue, there is both violence and imperialism at play when Western experts claim the license to generalise about, for example, 'the Muslim mind' (Waddy, 1991). To say that all people of the Islamic faith have the same attitudes is as offensive as saying 'all Christians are homophobic'.

Generalisations about groups of people are always misleading. Whether they are concerned with culture or religion, men or women, people with a mental illness, social workers, and so on, summary statements are distortions as such accounts inevitably simplify and standardise. This is an active conceptual operation, one that removes individuality and prescribes a narrow specificity of the person or group. This process of dehumanisation occurs with the respectable generalisations offered by the empirical sciences just as it does with folk statements uttered by the prejudiced. Mindful of this difficulty, practitioners can still use generalisations if they are employed tentatively. Generalisations can provide orientation, can act as a prompt for perspective-taking and

*This chapter was co-authored with Mark Furlong.

can offer specific reference points for the development of questions and comments.

As well as being sceptical about generalisations, insofar as we are person-centred in our practice we can actively reject the role of being an expert categoriser. It is appropriate for practitioners to see themselves as learners rather than as experts. If we understand that the people for whom we work are sentient and reflective, these people become mirrors upon which the practitioner has the opportunity to consider her or his own reflection. Although this relationship is always mediated by one's role and agency, in the practice space the professional is also a 'host': someone who should be a courteous, open-minded and sensitive listener (Cox, 1989). In this dual role we are both self- and other-oriented and 'the other' gives to us by offering assistance so we might better know who we are and where we come from, and what is our own culture, as well as offering prompts to help us grow into what we might become. Our work involves business relationships with our clients, but the exchanges we have with 'the other' (with those who present with differences that may be problematic or may be simply distinctive) contain complex elements.

With this as background we argue that an engagement with the question of marriages between Muslims and Christians offers a special kind of 'test site' for examining and appreciating the practices of difference. This is particularly the case given the troubled history between Muslims and Christians (Wheatcroft, 2003) because of our currently contested international politics: the so-called clash of civilisations (Huntington, 1993; Lewis, 1990). In this local test site, intimate relations engage with the geopolitics of difference, allegiance to the spiritual coexists with the daily demands of practicality and compromise, the private and public interpenetrate and jostle. Where could we find a more stimulating place for active listening and personal reflection?

The Current Exercise

This chapter sets out to offer a novel, albeit preliminary, contribution. It has both a 'research base' and a 'practice focus'. The primary author brings to the current project research that focused on collecting and analysing the responses of a sample of Australian people who are married and who have different religious faiths to their partners, specifically where one party has a self-declared Muslim faith and the other a Christian faith (Ata, 2003). The second author, who has an extensive background in teaching and practising casework, undertook the task of 'milling' the products of the empirical research, to refine the ideas relating to, and implications for, practice with those persons who are in, or perhaps who are contemplating being in, relationships with someone from a different faith.

In the following there are two sections. First, there is a brief summary of the initial research process and of the project's key findings. Second, four themes are presented that may have particular relevance for practitioners as reference questions. These four themes are: (a) differences in how the 'private and the public' divide is understood in Christian and Muslim understandings of marriage; (b) the idea that different participants, including workers, may operate from differing understandings of identity and selfhood; (c) particularly with respect to gender and how this may articulate with asymmetries of power and hierarchy, how should the worker deal with the question of alignment; and (d) should apparently religious differences be reframed.

Initial Research

Intermarriage can be characterised in a number of ways. Differing ethnicity, birthplace, race and status have been used as defining characteristics of intermarriage, particularly between host and immigrant groups (Penny & Khoo, 1996). Defining intermarriage for the purposes of the study was religious affiliation, that is, where one party was Christian and the other Muslim. This particular example of intermarriage overlaps with, but is not the same as examples based on contrasts of ethnicity, language, race or culture. Why did the current research concentrate on religion? One reason is that it has been argued that the guidelines for relationships are more clearly defined by religious doctrine than by the culture itself (Caltabiano, 1985). Another reason is that while there is some available literature examining religion and human service practice (Hodge, 2004; Loewenberg, 1988), cross-faith partnerships in themselves have not received such attention.

In order to examine this question an empirical project was designed. Data was derived from structured, face-to-face interviews. The majority of items on the interview schedule were 'close-ended' but the schedule also included a small number of 'open-ended' questions. After trialling invitations by letter, a 'snowballing' sampling design was eventually used to identify potential participants from an initial set of possible contacts offered through an informal network who shared with the researcher an interest in interfaith dialogue. All participants were drawn from the state of Victoria and were interviewed as individuals rather than as couples.

The final sample excluded those from arranged, mail order and 'shotgun' marriages. Participants could fall anywhere along the spectrum of religious adherence; that is, persons were not included on the basis of the frequency with which they observed religious rites and celebrations. Rather, inclusion was on the basis of self-defined theological identity. One hundred and six persons were interviewed and these people were drawn from 20 countries of birth. Presumably related to the pattern of men being more associated with the taking up of more public roles, the final sample was overrepresented in this group (63 men; 43 women), an occurrence that was not planned as part of the research design. The group comprised the following: 44 Muslim males, and 19 Christian males (total 63 males), and 33 Muslim females and 10 Christian females (total 43 females).

Further description of the sample, such as respective educational and employment status, patterns of 'drift' for partners into their spouses religious affiliation, birthplace, and so on, are detailed elsewhere (Ata, 2003).

Key Findings: Patterns of Response in Interfaith Marriages

Couples in mixed faith relationships report they have to contend with many challenges. For example, many respondents reported that they have experienced fraught reactions from relatives and friends, that they have become the focus for community concern, and that they have had to confront apparently incompatible religious expectations. Given such challenges, what determines whether these tensions will be inflamed or contained? Respondents discussed how particular variables potentiated or ameliorated these tensions, for example as related to the intensity of respective religious identifications, or as a consequence of a commonality, or a difference, with respect to language and aspirations.

As well as the challenges, respondents also reported a number of positive outcomes; for example, the idea that dealing well with religious differences can act to strengthen relationships. More generally, reading across the data generated in the interviews it appeared that there were discernible patterns in how couples evolved with respect to their different faiths. Sometimes these patterns seemed well thought through, sometimes interviewees reported patterns with mixed, perhaps even contradictory, features. Six patterns that were identified:

1. *Conversion or annexation.* This is where one party converts to the faith of the other. This was reported as either a positive and progressive choice or as a kind of co-option, an annexation ('You can't marry a chicken and a rooster.').

2. *Ignoring or withdrawing.* Here both parties withdrew from discussion of religious matters and enacted a de facto policy of ignoring (literally not speaking about) the question of religious difference. While this was reported as having some initial advantages, this style of adaptation was reported as producing difficulties in the longer term.

3. *An active policy espousing a plurality of faiths.* Some couples adopted an explicit policy of religious pluralism, perhaps both attending services in

turn or adopting a pattern of joint membership and participation. One respondent said 'it is a case of creating healthy boundaries ... of ensuring peaceful coexistence'.

4. *Compromising and negotiating.* This is a radical pattern where both parties leave their religion of origin and take up an 'in-between' allegiance. Although it appeared to be the way around 30% of the sample acted, it was apparently difficult for respondents to actively reflect on aloud in the interviews.

5. *Pastoral, ecumenical yielding.* Some interviewees reported that they actively attempted to 'merge' the rites and practices of their different faiths in their home. This may be done to a greater or lesser extent and, most likely, could act to forge a common ground even if problems might be encountered with respect to questions of coherence.

6. *Respect for 'otherness'.* In some respects this is similar to (3) above; some couples choose to individualise religious observations, that is, to have each person partake in her/his own way a religious life and to practice a respect for difference, neither attempting to coopt or minimise differences. As well as the expected advantage, some respondents suggested that this style risked companionship and was confusing to children.

A fuller account of these patterns can be inspected (Ata, 2003). A brief commentary on these patterns from the perspective of a practitioner is set out below.

Implications for practice

It is unlikely many caseworkers will see Muslim–Christian couples presenting directly for marital work. Yet, depending on the service, social work practitioners may have contact with one, or both, parties in a mixed faith relationship in may kinds of presentations. Contact with the couple can occur indirectly — one may have contact with these people in their capacity as parents, for example, in relation to one or more of their children if the worker is in a children's health or child protection setting. Agencies involved in generic 'problems of living', for example, around aged care or consumer debt, income security or community health, may have contact with one person in a couple. In these kinds of contacts practitioners can meet with a (potential) client only to find that the initial presenting problem that was thought to be about aged care or personal debt resolves into an issue of depression or grief, perhaps even directly into what the practitioner, if not the client, sees as the matter of 'relationship problems'.

If contact occurs, practitioners may find it helpful to review the above styles of adaptation and to use this material for its value as an aid to their personal thinking and/or in their direct discussion with the client. For example, one may ponder the question: 'What are the advantages and disadvantages of "withdrawing and ignoring" for this woman?' (see theme 2 above). Such a consideration may help one generate empathy and connect. Of course, this question could be discussed directly with the client and used as a starting point for discussion: 'Do you see that you and your partner have a way of doing things that is similar to a pattern that could be called "withdrawing and ignoring"?' Presumably, this would only be offered if the client and the worker did have a joint understanding that it was desirable to direct attention to the relationship itself. (The question of 'directness' is an important theme, one that will be specifically focused on later in this chapter.)

It could be expected that each of the above styles of adaptation has benefits and drawbacks. There are also challenges to be managed that arise with respect to unexpected crises, expected family life cycle transition points, and the obligation to observe key religious events. Distinct from these patterns, in considering the broader data, a number of themes were identified that practitioners might find useful as key reference questions and as particular points of orientation. Each of these four questions will be examined in turn:

1. **Views on marriage: Differences in how the 'private and the public' divide is understood and regulated**

If a couple is at odds, is this something about which respective fathers- in-law should know, perhaps even arbitrate about, or would this amount to an inappropriate intrusion? Should a daughter tell her own mother that her husband is a gambler, is impotent or violent or unfaithful? Is it shaming to a whole 'clan' if a one party in a couple wishes to talk to a counsellor, or a 'rival' religious figure, about a problem they might be having with a teenage son? Perhaps even more potentially dishonouring, what if one, or both, parties are having trouble resolving their own differences?

A theme that was present in several interviews was that Muslim marriages were more a 'public matter' than were Christian understanding of marriage. That is, there was a perception that third parties, such as family elders or religious authorities, were more likely to be seen to have an active role in Muslim marriages. Similarly, the matter of honour and shame was thought to be more a public issue in Muslim communities than in Christian settings. As with all such generalisations, there are many mediating factors in addition to religion and the degree of religious piety in play. For example, questions of educational level and those concerned with practicalities around housing arrangements are implicated in how the divide between the couple and their larger audience is understood and managed. This noted, the description that Muslim marriage had a more permeable boundary, that is, was more inclusive than Christina marriages is a view that is consistent with a seam of opinion in some literary, anthropological and therapeutic texts (Al-Krenawi, 1998; Al-Krenawi, Maoz & Reicher, 1994; Said, 2000).

Whatever opinions are put forward, it should be understood that all marital unions entail multiple stakeholders and involve third parties (Colgate, 2004) even if this complexity is less obvious in some cases. For example, Christian ministers may be ordained through their internal church processes but ministers have to be state registered to become licensed marriage celebrants. Similarly, divorce is a matter Western states reserve the right to govern and, at a different level, the law of the state is invoked if one party in a marriage is violent to their spouse. Put very generally, all couples may be subject to what their neighbours and local communities think; for example, some neighbours will contact the police if they believe that domestic violence is present. Therefore, it is incorrect to assert that Christian marriages do not have dynamic, formal relationships with their environments. For this reason it could be argued that the Muslim understanding of marriage as both a private and a public matter represents an honest and potentially progressive appraisal.

It may be that exchanges between the public and the private in Christian marriages are as frequent and as powerful as they are in Muslim marriages but that the former have a character that is more opaque than the latter. For example, the presence of patriarchy in the Christian church may be expressed in implicitly privileging practices (as well as in more obvious behaviours). In contrast, the involvement of third parties in Muslim marriages can be more prominent as their intercessions tend to be seen as being undertaken to further the interests of the male party. Clearly, this partial advocacy cannot be understood as purely a religious matter — cultural, sociolegal, geographical and historical factors would also be involved.

What is at issue for our current purposes is not whether there are exchanges between the private, 'couple-only' dimensions of marriage and the aspects of this union that are penetrated by 'third party' involvements. Rather, what may be experienced as difficult to those in interfaith unions is that there may be divergences: when is it proper to speak of a couple, or parenting-related difficulty and, if it is appropriate, to whom is it proper to speak? As is well known, it often risks stigma and shame to tell 'an outsider', even if this person has a professional qualification about a matter that might be framed (by one or both parties in the marriage or by one, or both, of their networks) as private or even 'spiritual.'

Implicated in this variable decision point are differences in beliefs about gender and gender roles where the question of religion and culture are closely entwined. The content of these beliefs is terrifically important and intensely emotive as they involve matters such as sexual faithfulness, infertility and domestic violence. Having an interest in how variably participants, including the practitioner herself or himself, prefer to define and manage the public or private divide in marriage can help practitioners orient their thinking in this difficult realm.

2. Understandings of identity and the self

A theme that was prominent in many interviews was that the quality of relatedness was especially valued. Moreover, this quality of perceived interdependence, of being other-oriented, of having an identity within a collective, tended to be shared between both Muslim and Christian respondents. Consistent with anthropological accounts of closely woven groups (Rapport & Overing, 2000), the theme of public face was also encountered. This occurred directly by way of statements about honour and reputation; it also occurred indirectly in the form of statements emphasising the importance of avoiding shame and social exclusion. Unlike the differences the research identified in assumptions about the public–private divide in marriage, which tended to be aligned with religious identification, in taking up a shared position on the importance of connectedness both sets of respondents could be said to contest the 'Western' assumption that the self is an island. It appears that interdependence was characteristic of the 'lived experience' (Schulz, 1972) of respondents.

This is a major issue for practitioners as current casework, counselling and mental health practice, like Western culture in general (Dumont, 1986; Heelas & Locke, 1981), tends to be premised on the supposedly inviolate (but in fact highly problematic) assumption that individuals are sovereign, unitary subjects (Furlong, 2003). This assumption creates difficulties because it generates a set of unhelpful conceptual and operational consequences for casework practice. Specifically, if each subject is assumed to be an independent entity this will have downstream effects that decisively, albeit opaquely, shape how the practitioner will think and act as it will determine how normality and wellbeing will be constructed. The well adjusted (the healthy and the functional) will be expected to be 'differentiated', 'individuated', self-determining while the poorly adjusted (the unhealthy and the dysfunctional) will be 'undifferentiated', 'fused' and 'dependent.'

Such constructions have particular consequences if the work is with persons with an identity that values interdependence. For example, most social work practitioners have been trained to engage in casework that uses orthodox microskills (Egan, 1990; Ivey & Ivey, 1999). These skills are premised on the work being framed in terms of the primacy of the individual client. Unfortunately, this frame is inconsistent with clients who are identified with (more) collectivist cultures. Insofar as the practitioner is individualistic rather than relational in the way their work is framed, this person will tend to assume the 'needs' of this client require attention. That is, this client needs to be empowered, facilitated to have firmer boundaries, assisted to be more self-managing, supported to be less prone to guilt, prompted to find greater personal fulfillment, and so forth.

What is of particular interest is not so much that parties in a couple may differ on how they think about and/or perform identity and selfhood, although this might be a source of tension. Rather, the issue may often be that the social work practitioner will tend to bring forward the received assumptions of their professional ideology that, as Meemeduma (1993) has argued, tend to reflect the 'Anglo' traditions of British and North American social work. Like the fish that cannot see the sea, if this is the case practitioners can implicitly reproduce in their actions and attitudes the Western assumption that identity and personhood is bounded by the skin. Insofar as a practitioner is working from this implicit position, this person will emphasise personal choice, entitlement and self-determination even if these 'principles' are not shared with one or both persons in the relationship with whom one is working.

3. *The question of alignment*
What gives the practitioner the cue to think about and to focus on matters to do with choice and individuality is that he or she will often encounter asymmetries in power and status as this relates to gender. The following section takes up this important matter as a priority that was not identified in the research per se but that arose in considering the research from the perspective of casework practice. That is, if one takes the research data and interrogates it for its usefulness to practitioners, a question is raised: how should the worker position themselves with respect to the presence of inequities as they relate to the linkages between gender and power?

Although there are often tensions in each episode of casework practice, the question of alignment arises as distinctly problematic in one particular class of presentations: how does one place oneself in presentations where the social position of women and men appears unfair, particularly with respect to differentials in power and status, equity and opportunity, which are based on gender when the purported rationale for this imbalance is religious? Clearly, this is an ethical and a technical matter, a question of both pragmatics and aesthetics, as it is also a trigger to strong feelings: asymmetries in relationships that conjoin gender with power are often emotionally evocative as they are interpersonally polarising. Like the immediate involved intimate participants, practitioners often endow these asymmetries with a defining significance. And this may be especially true if the social worker is a woman — that is, if the worker is someone who has directly experienced sexism.

Assuming that the couple is heterosexual, it follows that the faith and culture, gender and sexual orientation of the professional sets up a particular configuration in relation to the couple. Many practitioners might relate to the unhappy experience of sitting with, and being stumped by, persistent unfairness: 'This man is being outright unfair and his partner not only puts up with it, she uses the Bible to justify it!'. It follows that the apparent beneficiary in the relationship, who is usually the male, is experienced by the worker as 'wrong' or as 'backward' or as 'exploitative'; the apparent loser is seen as 'a victim', as 'brainwashed', as 'needing consciousness raising.' Without exhausting the many other permutations, a possibility here is that an 'Anglo' or 'Anglo-styled' practitioner can be triggered into the process of 'other-ing' as they are acting as if one, or both, their clients are not active and sentient subjects (Dominelli, 2002). If this occurs, the practitioner can lose empathy with, perhaps even dehumanise, one or both members of the asymmetric couple as a result of impotently confronting stubborn injustice.

Concurrently, one person in the couple, or perhaps both, may then 'other' the practitioner as the latter comes to be seen as discourteous, disrespectful, as foreign and no longer engaging. Perhaps such dynamics are implicated in the high drop-out rate of people from diverse backgrounds in their contact with 'Anglo' services. One study suggested this drop out rate was as high as 50%, as these one-visit shoppers did not return and noted that their experience of this contact was that it was insensitive (Adams & Gilbert, 1998).

Presentations where major social norms have been breached, such as domestic violence, need to be defined as unacceptable and prioritised as needing immediate attention. Yet, putting these breaches to one side, there are a larger set of presentations that feature asymmetries of power and status, which seem to expose apparently everyday privilege and unfairness. In this latter case it is largely the practitioner's agenda, their definitions, thresholds and sensibilities that are invoked and taken up as much, or more, than what the client presents.

Practitioners are never neutral and should not pretend to be. Yet, it is naive to believe that the simple declaration of one's position will always be received as courteous and engaging. Nor is it always the case that such declarations will facilitate the outcome that is desired. We have to think through this complication: sensitivity, as Cox (1989) notes, is the fundamental attribute for understanding how to practice in diverse communities. We wish to be sensitive, to proceed with care, yet this is not to avoid that which is difficult to say: it is central that we do not avoid direct discussion of, and negotiation about, key differences and difficulties (Miller, Donner, & Fraser, 2004).

What does one do as a practitioner if one party in a couple with whom one is working understands a problem — for example, difficulties with conception as an expression of God's plan, as 'divine will' or 'the consequence of sin' — and the other party thinks this is 'irrational, backwardly fatalistic'. Perhaps more troubling, what if both parties see this difficulty as 'God's way' but the practitioner thinks this is irrational and fatalistic? In all practice situations professionals have to make decisions as to how they will position themselves with respect to the 'presenting problem', a matter that is frequently defined and constructed asymmetrically between the participants, including the professional (Furlong & Lipp, 1995).

If we see ourselves as 'companions' and as 'hosts' to those with whom we work, if we see the work as a partnership rather than as 'acting on' the other, we have to be prepared to, perhaps even be observed to be, changing our own behaviour in order to build rapport and to gain trust. Couples in interfaith marriages are often engaged in ongoing dialogue and, even if this does not lead to an harmonious end, such exchanges are a contribution as this relationship is an engagement with living a life where a certain class of difference is a fundamental characteristic. Aligning with this ethic seems a fair aim.

4. Reframing 'religious differences'.

The research we have used in this chapter suggested that tensions in relationships were often reported to involve perceived struggles about religion. As one Malaysian man stated: 'I rarely felt I was concerned about declaring my religion back home, nor did I know much about it. I am much more aware of it and defensive about it in Australia than I ever dreamt of'. The current research echoed what Speelman (1997) and other investigators have suggested: partners in mixed marriages feel a deep need to be heard, understood and respected by the person of another faith whom they love. Indeed, this seems important, yet one may ask: isn't this theme always important given each of us, in terms of gender, background, is always 'from another planet' to one's partner?

This need for respectful connectedness can be seen as an underlying issue in any intimate, primary relationship. Yet, in an interfaith marriage the difference in religion is so centre-stage that it will tend to provide the readymade explanation for interpreting what stands behind any day-to-day tensions that may arise. Insofar as this occurs, there will be a tendency to focus on religious differences at the cost of properly considering other possibilities. Mindful of this pattern, practitioners may wish to consider reframing and redirecting controversy about perceived religious sticking points. As in work with 'ordinary' couples, simply recycling well-rehearsed themes can be unhelpful: every couple has a list of the 'usual suspects' that get rounded up when feelings are running high — for example, 'you men are all the same', 'I'm always putting the garbage out'. If your client is from an interfaith couple, it can sometimes be counterproductive to concentrate on religion as this can inflame righteousness. Perhaps, it may be better to decentre religious difference and to act towards reconnection and fluidity.

White (1986, p. 1) remarked that 'when partners in relationships are unable to suspend their belief that they have access to the sole truth … there are no grounds for the establishment of 'sensitivity' or 'being in touch' in their relationship'. Whether the source of this 'urgency for sameness' is purportedly doctrinal, or because it is concerns differences in gender or class, culture or personal history, the search for the 'deep appreciation of difference' remains the same quest. If this is so, why insist that one class of difference — the religious — has to hold the foreground?

Although it may sound strange, perhaps even contradictory given the focus of the research was on religion, we came to wonder: might it often be better if practitioners declined to focus on what seems like 'religious differences?' Might it be better to reframe out of differences that are embedded in stable, even rigid, oppositions of based on doctrine? Might not ascriptions of conflict based on religious faithfulness tend to lead to processes that inflame rather than resolve? And is it possible, indeed is it ethical, to attempt to cast the terms of the exchange into those that are more local, more fluid and less ossified than those that are intersectarian?

Calling to the Diversity in Diversity

If one is interested in culture, ethnicity and religion, where might one go for instruction? Is it best to consult the most recent empirical research texts or is seeking out practice wisdom the best path? The liberal tradition assumes the incremental education of those who are 'empty of knowledge' by those who are more objective and 'full of knowledge'. Put colloquially, this is the 'large jugs and small mugs' formula (Martin, 1998). Or one can seek out representatives of the groups one wishes to become knowledgable about and listen to these home-grown experts. Yet, however worthy, this later policy can also be risky as activists involved with the politics of identity movements, along with those having a poststructural bent, tend to assert that no-one has the right to speak for any other, including those from her/his own group.

Arguably, a commitment to respect and curiosity, to a thoughtfully 'not knowing' position (Anderson & Goolishian, 1988) may be more useful to practitioners than generalisations about the nature and ways of any particular 'diverse' group. Keenan (2004, p. 541) suggests that 'a stance of informed not knowing [is important so as to] mitigate against essentialism and stereotyping'. Similarly, and in a clear critique of those that urge practitioners to become 'culturally competent'.

Dean (2001, p. 624) suggests we celebrate one's lack of competence as integral to the gaining of an understanding:

> With 'lack of competence' as the focus, a different view of practicing across cultures emerges. The client is the 'expert' and the clinician is in a position of seeking knowledge and trying to understand what like is life for the client. There is no thought of competence, instead one thinks of gaining understanding (always partial) of a phenomenon that is evolving and changing.

And, as one reflects further, other complications arise. For example, practitioners who work with the individuals and families of those who are deemed 'other', and researchers who study individuals and families who are diverse, tend to have diverging interests as they conduct their respective practices in significantly distinct domains. Researchers wish to generalise, to 'discover' valid and reliable, broadly applicable truths; practitioners wish to do the opposite: to find singularities, to seek out particularity and possibility out of the general and the fixed. Such different perspectives mean that these two 'tribes' have different definitions of utility that, in turn, offers a degree of explanation as to why there is so little cross-citation, so little active consensus as to what is mutually relevant, between the texts concerned with family research and those texts written for practitioners who work with families.

Rather than the liberal or positivistic approach, the current chapter has taken a reflexive stance, that is, to literally propose that 'the other is a mirror'. Yes, it is helpful to have some conceptual architecture, some key reference questions that provide the practitioner with provisional ideas: about Indigenous people, about people with a mental illness, about Shia or Sunni Muslims. And it is important to have a critical approach that points to 'first world' premises as much or facts that claim to characterise and capture what 'they are like'. This acknowledged, we suggest that the casework task is also furthered by a stance that emphasises learning rather than knowing. If the client, the 'other', is considered from the existential starting point that this person is a sentient, reflexive being, it is clear that this offers a particular advantage: dialogue with this person creates the milieu within which one can better locate one's own cultural position. With this ethos one's work becomes part of one's struggle, one's encounters with awareness and reflection. Such a stance is also consistent with an understanding that one's work is not simply technical or instrumental, that it should not be considered non-missionary in nature. And, this can be exciting because, just maybe, 'we' are the weirdos here.

In commenting on slapstick comedy and its ability to offer deceptively strong insights, Barthes (1973, p. 44) wrote:

> (Charlie) Chaplin ... shows the public its blindness by presenting (on a stage) at the same time a man who is blind and what is in front of him. To see someone who does not see is the best way to be intensively aware of what he does not see.

Rather than assuming that practitioners should seek to be the expert on 'the other', the current contribution has been animated by the belief that practice with diverse clients puts our profession and broader culture on the stage. In such a viewing place what is contingent in our received practices and understandings is clearer. To a useful extent this may denaturalise some of what we take for granted, an outcome that offers the practitioner challenge and the opportunity for growth.

Acknowledgment

This research first appeared in *Australian Social Work* (vol 59, No. 3, 2006, pp.250-264): http://www.informaworld.com

References

Adams, C.E., & Gilbert, J.M. (1998). Providing effective counselling services to Australia's ethnic minority groups. *Australian Social Work, 51*(2), 33–40.

Al-Krenawi, A. (1998). Family therapy with a multi-parental/multi-spousal family. *Family Process, 37*(1), 65–82.

Al-Krenawi, A., Maoz, B., & Reicher, B. (1994). Family and cultural issues in the brief strategic treatment of Israeli Bedouin. *Family Systems Medicine, 12,* 415–425.

Anderson, H., & Goolishian, H. (1988), Human systems as linguistic systems: Preliminary and evolving ideas about the implications for clinical theory. *Family Process, 27*(4), 371–394.

Ata, A.W. (2003). *Christian-Muslim intermarriage in Australia*. Melbourne, Australia: David Lovell Publishing.

Barthes, R. (1973). *Mythologies*. London: Palladin.

Caltabiano, N. (1985). How ethnicity and religion affect attitudes towards mixed marriages. *Australian Journal of Sex, Marriage and the Family, 6*(4), 221–229.

Colgate, C. (2004). *Just between you and me: The art of ethical relationships*. Melbourne, Australia: Pan Macmillan.

Cox, D. (1989). *Welfare practice in a multicultural environment*. New York: Prentice-Hall.

Dean, R. (2001). The myth of cross-cultural competence. *Families in Society, 82,* 623–630.

Dominelli, L. (2002). *Anti-oppressive social work theory and practice*. Basingstroke, England: Palgrave.

Dumont, L. (1986). *Essays on individualism: Modern ideology in anthropological perspective*. Chicago: University of Chicago Press.

Egan, G. (1990). *The skilled helper: A systematic approach to effective helping*. Pacific Grove, CA: Brooks/Cole.

Furlong, M. (2003). Self-determination and a critical perspective in casework: Promoting a balance between interdependence and autonomy. *Qualitative Social Work, 2*(2), 177-196.

Furlong, M., & Lipp, J. (1995). The multiple relationships between neutrality and therapeutic influence. *Australian and New Zealand Journal of Family Therapy, 16*(4), 201-211.

Goldstein, H. (1983). Starting where the client is. *Social Casework, 4,* 267-275

Heelas, P., & Locke, A. (1981). *Indigenous psychologies: An anthropology of the self.* London: Academic Press.

Hodge, D. (2004). Developing cultural competency with evangelical Christians. *Families in Society, 85*(2), 251-260

Huntington, S. (1993). The clash of civilizations. *Foreign Affairs, 72*(3), 22-28

Ivey, A., & Ivey, M. (1999). *Intentional interviewing and counselling.* Pacific Grove, CA: Brooks/Cole.

Keenan, E. (2004). From socio-cultural categories to socially located relations: Using critical theory in social work practice. *Families in Society, 85*(4), 538-545.

Lewis, B. (1990). The roots of Muslim rage. *The Atlantic Monthly, 266*(3), 47-60

Loewenberg, F. (1988). *Religion and social work practice in contemporary American society.* New York: Columbia University Press.

Martin, S. (1998). *Adult learning and social work education.* Unpublished master's thesis, La Trobe University, Melbourne, Australia.

Meemeduma, P. (1993). Re-shaping the future: Cultural sense and social work. In J. Gaha (Ed.), *Proceedings of the 23rd Australian Association of Social Workers (AASW) Conference, Newcastle,* (pp. 163-167).

Miller, J., Donner, S., & Fraser, E. (2004). Talking when talking is tough: Taking on conversations about race, sexual orientation, gender, class and other aspects of social identity. *Smith College Studies in Social Work, 74*(2), 377-392.

Penny, J., & Khoo, S.-E. (1996). *Inter-marriage: A study of migration to integration.* Canberra: Australian Government Publishing Service.

Rapport, N., & Overing, J. (2000). *Social and cultural anthropology: The key concepts.* London: Routledge.

Said, E. (1978). *Orientalism.* London: Routledge and Kegan Paul.

Said, E. (2000). *Out of place: A memoir.* London: Granta.

Schulz, A. (1972). *The phenomenology of the social world.* London: Heineman.

Speelman, G. (1997, June). *Christian-Muslim marriages.* Conference paper presented at the European Ecumenical Assembly, Graz, Austria.

Waddy, C. (1991). *The Muslim mind* (3rd ed.). New York: Longman.

Wheatcroft, A. (2003). *Infidels: The conflict between Christendom and Islam 638-2002.* London: Viking.

White, M. (1986, Summer). Couples therapy: 'Urgency for sameness' or 'appreciation of difference'. *Dulwich Centre Newsletter, 1986/7,* 1-3.

Chapter 12

Opting for an Eschatological Interpretation
of Interfaith Marriages*

Interfaith marriage is a strong indicator as to whether a particular group is fully integrated into and accepted by the mainstream community. It is an eschatological vocation for today. As the desire to marry or be committed to a sacred relationship is being questioned, interfaith marriage challenges not only the rationalisation of marriage as a commodity to be consumed and enjoyed, but also national and cultural tendencies of totality and self-interest. There is nothing like an interfaith marriage to shock and rupture a nationalism bent on being 'for- and in-itself'. Being 'for-itself', nationalism signifies violence and death and, being 'in-itself', it can confuse the world with itself. In contrast, as a committed and intimate relationship, an interfaith marriage can indicate that absence of prejudice between members of the host and minority communities. This suggests that interfaith dialogue and tolerance are an integral part of two communities, as reflected within interfaith families.

When we look at an interfaith marriage, we have an opportunity to conceive of it as an encounter. Interfaith marriage is not just a personal experience of commitment, practice and mutual learning. Given that marriage is a sacrament in which God communicates divine grace, it is a space and time of an eschatological encounter with the person of Christ. Given that there is difference in unity in the Trinity, that is, an infinite openness of mutual divine giving and receiving between the Father and Son through the Spirit, we can imagine that such divine giving and receiving must overflow into the sacrament of marriage. The sacrament is a space of hospitality for the gift of love to be nurtured. Let us explore its meaning as the time of an encounter with the Otherness of Christ. The more marriage

*This chapter was co-authored with Glenn Morrison.

embraces difference-in-unity, the more an eschatological vocation might be lived. This suggests that interfaith marriage might offer possibilities for a Trinitarian praxis of otherness and mutuality. The key is to emphasise interfaith marriage as an encounter with God, the world and humanity rather than just limiting it to a personal and exclusive experience between a man and a woman. Interfaith marriage by virtue of its nature is not exclusive, but inclusive of God, the world and humanity.

However, full acceptance of interfaith marriage is not without trauma, humiliation and persecution. These are harsh realities. But, if truth is going to have its way in an interfaith marriage, meaning has to be found in suffering and sacrifice. We cannot just look at the dynamics of interfaith marriage objectively, as this would reduce any findings to theory and ideas. We have to come to an understanding that an interfaith marriage is about people and all their struggles and hopes. This suggests that meaning and truth can be discovered through the lens of ethical subjectivity.

When we consider ethics and subjectivity together, we see the drama of a developing life and moral conscience. This amounts to an eschatological vocation of holiness, a life of difficult freedom that demands great responsibility. With this in mind, we can begin to wonder what the state of interfaith marriage demands. It is a demand that no eye has seen nor ear heard nor human heart conceived. It can never be perceived for it is a sign of a trace of a divine gift like the vintage that has been maturing since the days of Creation. We can begin to imagine theologically that interfaith marriage is not necessarily like a new wine, but is an ancient, untouched wine full of promise for a world of unity-within-difference. This signifies that interfaith marriage is countercultural and counternationalistic tendencies. We can begin to see that the meaning of interfaith marriage rests on its vocation of being otherwise, being other-centred and being other-oriented. It is necessarily about an encounter that overwhelms what is seen or heard or experienced in the heart. But through time, through encountering the various forms of difference and otherness in each other, a sense is reached, a veritable transcendence in which the word of God is welcomed and transformed into hospitality, sacrifice and responsibility, to be passed on through the generations.

Some researchers have produced evidence that interfaith marriages will preserve and strengthen the boundaries of the individual's identity; others have argued that they will ultimately weaken and erode them (Quadagno, 1981; Stephan, 1989). Other studies have shown that it is possible to embody multiple identities, and that parts of one's customs can be preserved. Price (1993) studied intermarriage rates for the second generation of interethnic marriages and found that they were higher than the first generation by 10%

to 60%, depending on the type of ethnic community. We can interpret that there is a sense within human consciousness that seeks difference and embraces otherness. An interfaith marriage opens the outer limits for people to become even intercultural and international within their worldview. These are seeds to overcome political and social injustice. It is apparent that a loving and responsible relationship is a model for overcoming difference. In this regard, it follows that if religious difference can be met with truth and meaning by way of loving sacrifice and fidelity, we can begin to imagine what no eye has seen, or ear heard or heart conceived.

Religion as a Main Definer

The literature abounds with findings where spouses with differing religious backgrounds experience more conflicts than those with similar ones. The explanation is that the guidelines of relationships and the values underlying behaviour are more clearly defined by religion than by the culture itself (Caltabiano, 1985; Penny & Khoo, 1996).

However, studies carried out recently in the United States point to an increase in out-marriages, where ethnic, racial, or national barriers used to dominate. That is, these barriers are not as strong as they used to be. If, however, one of the partners displays a stronger religious behaviour, such as in dress, food use and other daily activities, tension between both partners tends to spiral. On the other hand, where tolerant religious behaviour is displayed between married partners, the relationship is obviously smoother.

For the Muslim community, religion takes on significant meaning. Religion and ethnicity are so closely linked that cultural adjustment between partners can be considerably more difficult to implement. This has manifested itself clearly not only in the Middle East but also among migrant Middle-Eastern communities in Australia (Ata, 1980).

For the majority of non-convert Muslims, religion is determined largely by ancestry, rather than personal conviction. Every respondent of the study identified his or her sectarian affiliation with the religion of his or her forebears. The main motive behind attending mosque did not seem to be any overwhelming personal belief, but rather confirmation of a distinct set of principles, such as lifestyle and social outlook, shared by co-religionists.

Interfaith marriages struggle with conflicts, heartache and trauma. The impact of one's religious–cultural–national identity on the self is a commanding one as it has been imprinted through the process of enculturation. It no doubt is a trauma for each spouse to confront and deal with difference. The ego's determination to capture the other to its own way of thought remains a constant temptation. If an eschatological vocation in the sense of achieving the impossible, namely a difference-in-unity, is to be lived, a sense of transcendence has to be developed and nurtured. If indeed religion is the defining factor that flows through the spirit, heart, mind and strength of one's being, there must be within oneself the trace of that ancient vintage that has been maturing since the days of Creation. What has always remained a primordial past has been the infinity of responsibility and peace. Religion, nurtured by spirituality, liturgy and wisdom, longs to drink of this pure vintage.

An interfaith marriage must embrace the drama of being faced with the other's difference. This involves not just listening to each other's fears and needs, but answering them. Again, this is a difficult freedom that considers the other's needs before one's own. The road towards responsibility and peace is a crooked one. Throughout life, the self is helplessly inundated with its own concerns, worries and fears. But, by facing the other spouse in an interfaith marriage, there is a hope that a sense of transcendence can be developed, where there has been a withdrawal of consciousness of concerns, worries and fears. In this radical turnabout from the ego, the self finds itself on the outside and in the world of the beloved.

A Look at Interfaith and Interchurch Marriages

Couples in interfaith marriages are often engaged in ongoing dialogue, not necessarily leading to a harmonious conclusion. But, like other monoreligious, monocultural marriages, being in such a relationship is in itself a contribution, an engagement in living a life together, and figuring out how to deal with issues as they arise. Crossing swords can imply a struggle resulting from power factors at work. The case involving a Christian woman married to a Muslim man is self-validating. Not only are the cultural backgrounds recognisably different, but the power basis and support reference are structurally different. This inequality translates identically into Western societies like Australia. Studies from the Australian Institute of Family Studies have shown that Australian women are discontented with the discrepancy in power resources between themselves and their partners.

Unlike their interfaith married counterparts, they may not discuss how to deal with pressures from their own communities, how to suppress socialised cultural values that inevitably clash with those of their partners, and if their children are to be swayed to their way of thinking. The main struggle underlying any type of marriage is what happens after a relationship of love and respect takes into account differences of world views, affective inclinations, and interpretation of events.

More often interfaith couples are seen as representatives of their particular communities. The Middle-Eastern husband is seen as a traditionalist who constantly has to explain the 'backwardness', 'intolerant' and 'intemperate gesticulating' movements of his compatriots and leaders of his country of origin. The Australian wife is a less reserved, opinionated creature from a superior culture — one who is particular about hygiene, environmental care, house and pet care and the like.

Often the tension reflects the depth and manner each partner identifies with her or himself. Their identity is clear to them so long as they look for ways to maintain it: how to keep their basic convictions, what things have worked for them in drawing intimacy and respect from others, how they negotiate with those whose way of thinking is different, and so on. Price (1993, 1994) and other ethno-demographers found that partners in mixed marriages feel a deep need to be heard, understood and respected by the person of another faith whom they love. The basis for self-hood is conditioned in all of us as we strive to build a better image of ourselves; a sort of self-recognition and self-respect. Accusations along the lines of, 'If you don't respect what I say and what I believe, you don't love me' are routinely heard in marriage counselling sessions and family courts in Australia.

One of the defining factors of the sense of identity is the religious traditions of Christians, Muslims, Jews, Bahai's and others. At a subconscious level the religious traditions thread in the cultural values adopted. We continue to negotiate and renegotiate our identity to keep altered ways of recognising others at bay, and to safeguard ongoing relationships. This is the reason for complicated struggles between mixed-faith couples.

The tension in the relationship arising from this situation often descends into a struggle about religion. When one party feels they are pushed onto the margins of the relationship, they overcompensate for the lack of respect by stressing what is most sacred to them: religion. A Malaysian man stated, 'I rarely felt I was concerned about declaring my faith back home, nor did I know much about it. I am much more aware of it and defensive about it in Australia than I ever dreamt of'.

Speelman (1997) believes that some couples in Muslim–Christian marriages say that they predominantly believe in the same sets of values, but not all. Others say that what they believe is not the same thing, although their faiths point in the same direction. It is of utmost importance that such couples accept and embrace that they do not believe the same ideas, instead of trying to bury their differences. This was confirmed by a Dutch-born woman who did not want to recognise the serious communication problem in her relationship because she was determined to prove to those who said it would never work that her marriage was fantastically successful. She and her partner had put off talking about their problem until it was too late.

Why is this insight important? In a pluralistic society like ours, Speelman (1997) observes that we have to learn to live together in spite of our differences and without feeling threatened. It is a way of finding how to live together in a win–win situation. Both partners must feel they are being taken into account, that what they regard as central to their life is being respected as sacred by their partner. We find here the beginning of an eschatological vocation. However, one that goes beyond dialogue must not take root in the ground 'of agreeing to disagree', that there are differences demanding impersonal tolerance and acceptance. The idea of 'beyond dialogue' is one that stretches the limits of the impossible. Dialogue, through words and meetings, will only achieve what is indeed possible. But human life is paradoxical and mysterious. We are not just content with what is possible. We want to be great and achieve the impossible. To go beyond dialogue in the context of an interfaith marriage ruptures the idea of the self and its tendency to be-for-itself. To go beyond dialogue is to be 'an Other'. In an interfaith marriage, this is to be in each other's skin. This may entail not just listening to the other spouse, but seeing and hearing what is beyond being seen and heard in consciousness, namely the word of God. Interfaith marriage is an ancient gift and if its vintage is to be beheld in its true eschatological splendour, then both spouses must be beholden to each other with a love stirred by a liturgy of responsibility and sacrifice.

References

Ata, A. (1980). Marriage patterns among the Lebanese community in Australia. *Australian and New Zealand Journal of Sociology, 16,* 112–113.

Caltabiano, N. (1985) How ethnicity and religion affect attitudes towards mixed marriages. *Australian Journal of Sex, Marriage and the Family, 6,* 221–229.

Penny, J., & Khoo, S.-E. (1996). *Intermarriage: A study of migration and integration.* Canberra, Australia: Australian Government Publishing Service.

Price, C., (1993). Ethnic intermixture in Australia. *People and Place, 1,* 6–8.

Price, C., & Zubrzycki, J. (1962). The use of intermarriage statistics as an index of intermarriage. *Population Studies, 15,* 58–69.

Quadagno, J. (1981). The Italian-American family. In C. Mindel, C. (Ed.), *Ethnic families in America: Patterns and variations* (pp. 61–85). New York, Elsevier.

Speelman, G. (1997). *Christian Muslim marriage.* Paper presented at the Graz European Ecumenical Assembly, Utrecht University.

Stephan, C., & Stephan, W. (1989). After intermarriage: Ethnic identity among mixed-heritage. *Journal of Marriage and Family, 51*(2), 507–551.

www.ingramcontent.com/pod-product-compliance
Lightning Source LLC
Chambersburg PA
CBHW071847230426
43671CB00012B/2088